Lightworker Within

Thought-Provoking Collection
from
Female Ascended Master Teachers

Ageless Wisdom Evolving Series

Astral Plane Revisited
    Master Djwhal Khul and the Cosmic Mentors

Initiations and Masters – Revised and Clarified
    Master Djwhal Khul and the Cosmic Mentors

Reincarnation – Earth and Elsewhere
    Connecting Evolution, Soul and Body, Earth and Beyond
        Master Teachers Kuthumi and Djwhal Khul with
        Off-Earth Allies Omstara, Philohstan and Sartarius

Books by Sharon K. Richards

Voices for the Ascended Masters
    – Masters don't view channeling the way we do
Word Songs from my soul – I
Word Songs from my soul – II

Copyright © 2020 Sharon K. Richards
All Rights Reserved.

ISBN: 9798604386651

Ageless Wisdom Evolving
Compilation from 21st Century Teachings

Lightworker Within

Thought-Provoking Collection
from
Female Ascended Master Teachers

Quan Yin
Mother Mary
Omstara
Lady Nada

Compiled & Edited by

Sharon K. Richards

CONTENTS

DEDICATION vii
PREFACE ix
ACKNOWLEDGEMENTS xi
INTRODUCTION xiii
FEMALE MASTER TEACHERS SPEAK xvii

QUAN YIN

Quan Yin Bio 3
Many Traditions – Many Gods 5
Wasteland in the Heart 7
The Seed of Fear – Your Greatest Enemy 9
The Joy of Living in Awareness 12
Balance is Balance 15

MOTHER MARY

Mother Mary Bio 21
Changing One's Image 23
The Real Message in My Life as Mother Mary 25
Spiritual Enfranchisement 29
On Prayer 33
Soul Evolution 37
All We Ask Is That You Listen 41
We Come By Request Only 45
Many Traditions – Many Gods 49
Facing the Challenge of Expanding Consciousness . 53
Together We Love 57

Working Together 61
Planting the Seeds of the New Earth 63
Mother Mary's Year-End Message 65

OMSTARA

Omstara Bio... 69
Adventures in Spiritual Growth.............................. 71
Working Together 73
Experience the Hidden Bond 77
Open Heart and Mind to What Will Be 81
What Limits Have You Set? 85
Pillars of Belief 87
Not Your Traditional New Year's Resolutions.......... 89

LADY NADA

Lady Nada Bio... 93
Consciousness 95
Soul Evolution 99
The Vital Role of Gender Equality......................... 103
Many Traditions – Many Gods.............................. 107
Street Fighting and the New Civilization............... 111
Compassion Unites the Human Family 117
Together We Love 121
Planting the Seeds of the New Earth 123
The Joy of Living in Awareness 125

ACCESS TO ADDITIONAL INFORMATION 129
About the Editor 131
GLOSSARY... 133

DEDICATION

The Lightworker Within is the voice of our Higher Self that supports us and asks us to walk in light and love and respect. Respect and concern include ourselves and every being within our awareness, be they intimate family, fellow shoppers in a checkout line or those unknown to us that we learn of via the news.

The Lightworker Within is the voice within that listens to heart wisdom and implements with heart-mind
- caring for the whole,
- choosing soul-based love before bristling with anger that stokes hatred,
- making decisions that at the end of the day, the week, the year, leave consciousness expanded and leave this world somehow a better place than it was a day, a week, a year ago.

The Lightworker Within hears the voice of personal guides, seeks to grow spiritually in the midst of life's daily challenges and responds to the work and opportunities that arrive on the doorstep.

May you find this collection to be a treasure trove of articles to enrich the Lightworker Within you.

Sharon K. Richards
Editor

PREFACE

This book gathers and brings forward observations, encouragement, explanations, advice, wisdom and warnings from four female Ascended Master Teachers. Each teacher has her own section.

Quan Yin, Mother Mary, Omstara and Lady Nada each look over my shoulder as I suggest the order of articles within their section. While in general I sought to create a harmonious message sequence, you can open the book at any page and let your guides – or the Lightworker Within – pick the place to begin.

Not every message will engage every reader. It is my hope that you will pick and choose, that you will find messages within these pages to enrich your journey.

You might ask why this sequence of speakers. I, too, asked. This was not the first sequence I explored. Yet, like so many decisions one makes when interacting with spirit, the sequence came to me and I knew it was the one to use.

Let this book be one that you pick up and set down, bring out and then tuck back on the shelf . . . until once again you are reminded that it is there.

It has been my sincere pleasure to assemble this collection. May it be your pleasure to browse, choose from and read.

In Light and Service,

Sharon K. Richards

ACKNOWLEDGEMENTS

None of the articles in this book would even exist were it not for the trust and determination of 25+ beings who no longer incarnate in the dense physical but rather advise and guide from beyond the veil. Each of these beings is further along the journey of return to Source than are the members of the incarnate production team they chose to work with in order to deliver their messages via the Internet.

None of the articles would exist without the dedication of the WeSeekToServe production team. This team has ranged from one to six individuals over the years and as of this writing, is four workers strong, each committed to continued publication of the Master Teachers' messages.

And none of articles would have been assembled without the trust and approval of Quan Yin, Mother Mary, Omstara and Lady Nada.

With deep gratitude to all,

Sharon K. Richards

INTRODUCTION

It has been my privilege to work with each of the female Master Teachers represented in this collection. All articles were channeled by myself or my colleagues and appeared in one of three Internet formats that were commissioned by Ascended Master Teachers.

Websites

ThoughtsFromAMaster.com was requested by Master Teacher Yeshua (Jeshua / Jesus of Nazareth). It launched in 2011 and ceased monthly publication after December of 2013. The site provided essays from Yeshua and commentaries in response to readers' questions.

Today, the site is a repository of teachings that are easily accessible by year of publication and by general topic.

WeSeekToServe.com launched in 2011. This site was requested by a team of Ascended Master Teachers in order to provide a platform where they could have panel discussions. Their objective was to provide a variety of perspectives on a single topic. They later added an Open Forum option where each teacher could speak to the topic of their choosing.

Publication ceased after the Winter 2017 issue. Today, the site is a repository of English messages, accessible by year of publication. It also stores bios for all 25+ contributors as well as profiles of the channeling team.

WeSeekToServe.org is today a companion repository for Spanish translations.

Facebook

The *WeSeekToServe Facebook* page launched in 2015 and is active today. All postings are bilingual, in English and Spanish.

Newsletter

The bilingual *WeSeekToServe newsletter* launched in 2018 and is active today. The newsletter usually contains four articles per issue.

The English newsletter sign-up can be found on *WeSeekToServe.com*.

The Spanish newsletter sign-up can be found on *WeSeekToServe.org*.

Bios and Icons

We on the WeSeekToServe team realized that there is a plethora of biographies available on the Ascended Masters. So we asked each contributor to comment on their current work and to relate a favorite or formative past life so that readers could get to know them better.

Just as there are many biographies, there are many images of the teachers. One of our editors suggested providing a graphic of the teacher's choice rather than a portrait. The contributors agreed. Each one explained what they wanted in a graphic and why they chose that image. One of our editors sought appropriate graphic options.

The teachers reviewed the options . . . and did not always select the graphic we editors preferred!

The icons and biographies for Quan Yin, Mother Mary, Omstara and Lady Nada appear at the beginning of the section that contains their articles.

Words and Perception

As you explore the articles in this collection, you will note that key terminology evolved between January 2012 when publication began and December 2019, the date of the last extract in this book.

The 19th and 20th century writings of the Ascended Master Teachers spoke of "the Hierarchy" or "the Spiritual Hierarchy." They spoke of "Ascended Masters," "Masters of Wisdom" or simply "Masters." This terminology continues to be used in many esoteric circles today.

However, the Ascended Master Teachers who spoke through the publications listed above, as well as the *Ageless Wisdom Evolving – Updated for the 21st Century* series of paperbacks and e-books, requested that established terminology be allowed to evolve. They wished to present fewer linguistic barriers between us and them and to more accurately reflect their planetary role and their relationship to 21st century humanity. Two terms were affected by this request:

Hierarchy

In 2013, Masters who contributed to WeSeekToServe requested that the channels who provided them with voices to the world begin to use the term "Community" rather than "Hierarchy." The Masters felt that "Community" better represents their relationship to one another. They felt that the term "Hierarchy" tends to imply a ruling authority that does not exist. They consider themselves to simply be elder brothers and sisters further down the spiritual path.

Ascended Masters

In his 2017 book, *Initiations and Masters*, volume 2 of the *Ageless Wisdom Evolving* series, Master Teacher Djwhal Khul explains that the term "Master" was initially meant to convey the teaching aspect of their work but over time had come too often to imply demi-god superiority. He explained that he and his colleagues preferred the title "Master Teacher" to "Ascended Master." We who channeled them respected that request and began to refer to them as Master Teachers.

Caveats

Because the teachers work as a team, you will occasionally find that the articles you're reading refer to articles and/or colleagues that are not represented in this collection. I handle each of these references separately with the objective of maintaining maximum coherence in the current article.

You will find my personal comments scattered throughout the book, box-outlined so that they can be easily identified and read or ignored as you choose.

From my Heart

Caveats aside, this book is the manifestation of a dream from my heart. I hope you find here a reservoir of insights to take into meditation . . . or to take into your life.

With love and blessings,

Sharon K. Richards

FEMALE MASTER TEACHERS SPEAK

QUAN YIN

Quan Yin focuses on the patient, compassionate healing of relationships that have been long fractured. Her specialty is Earth's relationships with our space brethren.

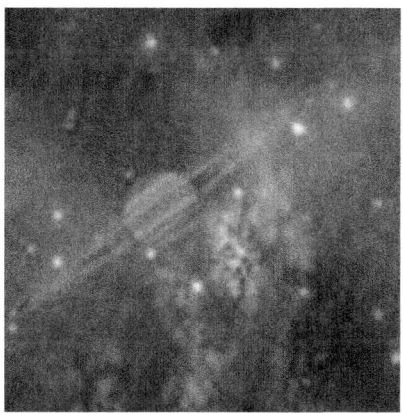

My Icon

I said, "I would like a planet, I'm thinking of Saturn, with stars in the background. That I would like." The icon chosen is precisely what I had envisioned. You see, it is the relationships with our distant space brethren that must be restored as well as relationships here on Earth. And what could be more distant to the human mind than the stars of deep space?

That is how some see the healing of old enmities – as distant as the stars. Yet they are also in close relationship in that they are grouped together, they are a cluster you could say. They stay in the same environment and thus must learn to not pollute one another as this also pollutes themselves. I try to show this relationship and use this logic to "crack open" the heart for all to understand how connected each is to the other.

Quan Yin has chosen carefully the panel discussions she wishes to join.

She is generally known for her compassion and wisdom. Yet in my experience, the other Master Teachers call on her when there are cultural disagreements with deep, firmly-held beliefs and expectations on each side. She is clearly respected by her colleagues

We who channel for WeSeekToServe articles receive assignments from the Master Teachers and I always look forward to the articles she channels through me.

Quan Yin Bio

Current Focus

My specialty is the healing of relationships, the healing, particularly, of relationships that have been long fractured, and more especially, those with our space brethren, for space brethren are not the alien enemies that are portrayed in so many movies. They are, rather, friends – friends come to assist Mother Earth. They come as friends to assist humanity.

When friendships have been long fractured, as they have been with our space brethren since the ancient times of Atlantis, it takes great determination, great patience and great diplomacy to rebuild trust. This is a position I enjoy greatly, for reunion is a step towards a greater good.

Favorite or Significant Past Life

One significant past life of mine occurred early in my soul maturity as soul maturity goes. And I was a young girl, and this was China. I learned as that young girl, I learned about pain when my feet were bound. I learned about the perverse ways that society declares what is beauty and what is not. Yet I knew in my heart that beauty had little, if anything, to do with the body I was in or with my feet.

And this is the wisdom and the lesson that I have taken with me as I deal in other lives – as I deal with those who are "too this," or "not enough that," too much of this or not enough of that, labels we use for each other based solely on physical characteristics. That lesson was seared very deeply into my view of what it means to have a human existence, and what it means to have a spiritual life.

I learned the importance of what you can call the Christ Consciousness within, as an expression of the Creator or of the Divine, for it is that beauty only that counts. And that beauty expresses itself in the way you interact with each other and with Mother Earth.

All that I learned at a very early age in a life when my feet were bound.

That would be my life. And that is what inspired me, I

think, to focus so much on healing relationships, for I had many relationships to heal based on my reactions to that life.
    I thank you.

> *To many, Quan Yin has become a virtual demigod. She comments on the path that brings her – and others – to that status. Mother Mary and Lady Nada also spoke on this panel.*

Many Traditions – Many Gods
WeSeekToServe.com Panel Discussion, May 2012

Quan Yin

I have much to say on this topic . . . and I have little to say on this topic. For you see, where does being honored and revered and respected, or in reverse order, respected and honored and revered, slip into being worshipped? Being deified? Where does that happen along the spectrum?

I would say I do not know at what point, and I don't think it is a point. It is not a line that is crossed. It is not a point that once you get there everything changes. It is more a mental journey and you do not realize that the context has changed until you are very deep into the new context. The change is so gradual it is not recognized. It is very likely not recognized within the person who is doing the respecting, the honoring, the revering, the deifying. And it may not be noticed by those who are outside watching others slide across that path or slide down that slope, whichever analogy you choose to use. I will pick one.

There was a fork in the river of relationships. It is relationship issue. And there is, let us say, a river, and this river is relationships. And this river is the relationship with me.

There are those who travel the river whose attention is not clear for various reasons, most of which is living in the dense physical plane in day-to-day life. And this river of relationship that existed in the emotions and in the mind, in this river there was a fork. One way, the relationship remained one of respect and honor. And in the other fork, there were a few more rapids and it became respect, honor, revere, deification – danger, rapids.

I am not deified. That says it all.

But this is not something that happens full blown all at once. It is simply a slippery, tricky course that must have attention paid to it so that it does not slip into the deification channel of the river, but stays, as it should, with respect.

How does it stay with respect? And honor, even? I will allow that.

That can be best expressed if lives such as mine are viewed simply as an example. As my colleagues have said, this life serves simply as an example. My story is an example of what *you* can do, of what you can be for each other. It is an example.

That is where I would have myself and my life as Quan Yin placed – an example to be emulated in whatever way possible in your daily life.

My message was simply to be an example, a human example, a human being as an example of what one human being can do and be for another in ways that are very, very small, but very, very, very meaningful.

Thank You,

Quan Yin

> *Quan Yin speaks strongly of the wasteland that can invade one's heart. She speaks of compassionate discourse with oneself – and offers her hand to those wishing to escape that wasteland.*

Wasteland in the Heart
WeSeekToServe.com Panel Discussion, October 2013

Quan Yin

A wasteland in the heart of any person is a devastating state, especially when there is always another manner of looking at life, another manner of living life. For a healthy person does not suffer from tendencies to live their life like this; they do not allow such static thinking to enter and stain their state of mind and lead to the downfall of the heart.

We, I, offer that a stance of compassionate discourse with oneself will rid one of the unworthy emotions and thoughts that may plague the heart and mind to turn against itself.

Self-worth is extremely important to the development of the soul, for without this self-worth, the heart and mind list and lag like a ship on a stormy sea. To "anchor one's heart" or to "firmly root one's feet" are both terms of great necessity.

We, I, recognize the epidemic of humanity who live this way in these days. Wasted hearts have always been apparent with some through the ages, but these days the gap has widened amongst those who feel this way about life in general and themselves in general. It will be difficult to engender a point of view to build a new and better future when one rests on their laurels or grovels in their own personal wasteland.

We as a team strive to uplift those who hide in this shadow, for without this uplifting they cannot see hope past stumbling in their own personal hell. This suffering, at best, is often an unnecessary, self-inflicted condition of confinement to a mental, emotional state that leaves an otherwise perfectly capable soul spinning its wheels. There is no time left for capable souls to remain trapped. Evolution is speeding up and time will stand still for no one. No one.

It is evident that many do not understand or care about

the fact of evolution has begun to accelerate. But once fate unfurls its sails, they will soon ponder with wider eyes and inquisitive minds as to just what is really going on.

I offer my hand to those who will strive now to unfurl their brow and open their hearts to new and brighter possibilities. You have the means to reach me.

Just ask and I will answer your call. Humanity is not alone. We, I, am here to help guide you, to chaperone you as an older sister, and it is my pleasure to do so.

Thank you.

Quan Yin

> *Taken together as one message with two parts, the next two articles expose the depth of Quan Yin's compassion for our well-being and our spiritual growth.*
>
> *Lady Nada also spoke on the panel for the second of Quan Yin's companion articles, "The Joy of Living in Awareness."*

The Seed of Fear – Your Greatest Enemy

WeSeekToServe.com Panel Discussion, May 2015.

Quan Yin

Fear is a topic very dear to my heart. I have observed over millennia the ever-growing tendency of humanity to allow fear to enter their domain. The human family is very prone to fear as a major self-created and easily accepted hindrance in their personal development as well as the development of groups and nations.

What is the origin of fear? It is obvious to me that in human evolution there is a link between the development of the human mind and the development of fear. The stronger the mind becomes, the greater the fear that is created. The mind is very much attached to the physical world, hence the importance of physical well-being.

Well-being for many is connected to possessions – be it the accumulation of physical goods or recognized status. There is individual status, group status and national status just to name a few, and each status seems to require an immense amount of safe-guarding. This constant safe-guarding is creating more and more levels of fear and insecurity.

There is, for individuals, status of family background, status of education, status of financial wealth, status and recognition of membership within the hierarchy of any given organization, status of the circle they mix and mingle with socially, and not to forget their physical possessions. All this and more seems to be so important that people feel obliged to protect their identified and affiliated statuses and material goods. This protecting is becoming increasingly stressful and creating fear on many different levels.

Then there is group status with multi-generational families of wealth or influence, prestigious schools, elite social clubs, companies of wealth and market share. These institutions are very keen to protect their achieved wealth and status, expecting each member to give their full support. And so there grows another level of stress and fear of losing status, membership or access to this sparkling environment.

Yet more comprehensive is national and international status of a country. This status lies with the various systems the country has put in place to function and be successful, starting with the legal framework that covers law and order for a variety of scenarios. The infrastructure within a country, from banking to schooling to transport to the production of goods and services, plus the process of interacting appropriately with neighboring countries and the world at large represent many more facets of the different statuses that a nation is engaged in defending. And again, there is the collective seed of fear of losing national achievement if one facet loses its sparkle.

Fear individually and nationally have taken a big toll on humanity. Those who are aware of this treadmill of fear want to get off, want to warn others of the danger fear carries.

Fear.

I ask you, "What is the worst thing that can happen to you?" This question is one of the keys to walking the middle path as a human being and learning to control or even neutralize fear.

Ask yourself the following questions to find out how you perceive fear:
- Is the physical world all there is?
- How dependent have I become on the physical world?
- How much have I already morphed into the role of slave to the physical world, turning one or even two blind eyes to the fact that I am a spiritual being having a physical experience at the moment?
- How far down am I on the path to fear?
- Can I stop and turn around?
- What are my biggest fears?
- And why?

And take into account that you are part of a network, a worldwide network, an intergalactic network. Fear of loss as it prevails on Earth is not part of the intergalactic network. It was Earth-developed, Earth-made. It is a feature that has slowly developed over millennia as different races who roamed this planet sank into the dense physical, developing the mind, the ability to rationalize, the survival instinct. Fear now goes hand in hand with features that developed in tandem with mind and survival, like ego, greed, hunger for power, lust for dominance over one another and the like.

Fear has also become a controlling tool whereby certain individuals or groups subjugate those who are weaker. Over thousands of years, the fear of being hurt physically, emotionally, mentally, spiritually, financially and/or politically has become part of the evolutionary cycle, part of Earth's "reincarnation package."

Yet as many historical events show clearly, if fear and threat, combined with ego and power hunger, had not been part of the game, a peaceful cohabitation of different parties around the world would have been easily possible.

Fear is a deal-stopper on your evolutionary path. Fear slows you down. Fear blocks you off.

You are eternal beings. It is time to let go of fear of the physical. There will always be unexpected events in life. Do not fear them. Welcome them as learning tools that will move you forward. Learn to distinguish between need and want in the physical world. Learn to see and think with your heart. Accept the fact that you are a spiritual being who has been granted a physical incarnation on planet Earth with all its earthly features. Enjoy that gift whole-heartedly and use it wisely.

When you find yourself in a fearful mindset, try to think with your heart. Your heart is the link to the intergalactic network. Your individual perceptions are released to the intergalactic network and through that network, experiences are shared and made known. Ask yourself therefore what you wish to put into a network that is accessible to the intergalactic community.

Do you want your fellow community members to experience fear? You have so much more power and so many more talents that would be of value to others.

Fear is not an attribute to be kept or shared.

Where there is fear, many imbalances are created and we need to heal from our side. When you, our brothers and sisters, are in balance, you and we can collectively collaborate to implement the divine plan. Let us collaborate fearlessly.

Take control, be bold. You have our full support.

The Joy of Living in Awareness
WeSeekToServe.com Panel Discussion, June 2015

Quan Yin

Joy is the radiance of the soul but it needs to be cultivated like a rare and beautiful flower. You must protect and nurture joy, you must invite it in and deeply experience its magical presence in your life. Rich, poor, old or young, you are all capable of this deep emotion called joy when you touch your soul and feel its signature there. And yet, for so many of you, so few are the moments spent in joy.

Why is this? Why should this be so?

Might I suggest that many of you spend much of your time and your being cloaked in fear – fear of want, fear of loss or abandonment, fear of what has been or what might befall, and almost universally, fear of change and the Great Unknown that change harbors. And so, though joy shines upon all like the radiant, generous sun, for many it is mostly unattainable, rarely experienced, fleetingly glimpsed.

Why is this, why should it be so, when joy could be the baseline of your life? Do you pay attention to it, do you listen for its deep call, or are you mostly numb? Worse yet, do you turn your back on joy and run from it for fear it will desert you?

Joy is like a rare and beautiful flower. You must protect and nurture it, with all your being and all your becoming, too.

And how do you become more joyful, how do you become Joy and let it fill your days?

By sharing it, sharing it full out. Share with friends and loved ones who will blossom too in the presence of your joy, but even strangers on the bus or in the streets and buildings where you pass will be touched by its subtle radiation. All of nature will share and reflect back to you its joy in sensing yours. You can touch the flowers, you can touch the stars, even if there is no one special in your life at the moment.

Joy is like a rare and beautiful flower. Invite it, coax it into your life to protect and nurture and share. And we will be with you, we who love and guide you, for in touching the joy in your soul, you open the door to our joyous reunion and embrace.

Ever lovingly yours,

Quan Yin

> *Quan Yin expresses the need for wisdom and patience when, as in many areas today, long-established inequalities are being rectified. She specifically requested the graphics in this article.*

Balance is Balance

WeSeekToServe Newsletter, September 2018

Quan Yin

Hello to the readers of this newsletter.

I am pleased to bring you a message, a concept that is very important to me. My area of expertise is bridging between Earth and civilizations off Earth. I work to heal and improve relationships between us, so I suppose you can categorize me as a diplomat.

I present the most positive image I can of planet Earth, all the while being honest from my heart about that which is positive, that which is working in light and that which is moving toward the light as well as that which is stuck. It is very easy for civilizations off Earth to hear stories of negative impressions or unpleasant experiences from those who have visited Earth. We quickly gain a dark reputation.

In other instances, civilizations off Earth remember historic incidents or situations and have simply checked us off the visitation list, never to return. This is not beneficial for anyone. So I attempt to repair and heal relationships long broken. That is what I do.

Those of you without experience off Earth would be astonished at how surprised distant cultures can be at the distinctions made on Earth between the two genders. Many civilizations have gender, yet for them, gender is no more noteworthy in behavioral expectations than is the color of one's eyes or the length of one's fingers. Their concept of equality/inequality is quite different from ours on Earth.

By equality I mean respect for skills and roles, respect for intellectual capability, respect for leadership capability, skills in decision-making, in diplomacy. On Earth, as a significant imbalance begins to rectify, the danger becomes leaning the scale entirely the other way.

"Before"   Can become "After"

Reversed inequality is often a stage in any circumstance where equality has been long denied, where one side of the scales has been long sloping low to the ground and the other side forever above. As that inequality begins to balance out, the danger is that there is a complete flip the other way. Those who did not have power swing high and wish to make up for the imbalance that has existed perhaps for decades, perhaps for centuries. Those from the low side of the scales too often feel that by now being dominant, they can quickly correct all the indignities left over from times when the balance was not in their favor.

But you see, balance is balance.

The wise ones who lead the way to retribution look at equality and balance, not dominance reversed. Balance is balance: equal distance from the ground or from the height on each side of the fulcrum. Balance is balance. Whether the inequality be wealthy and impoverished, gender, power and impotence, philosophical and religious beliefs, economic structures, balance is balance.

Balance is not those who have been downtrodden and

ignored gaining supremacy and turning the other side into the downtrodden and ignored. Balance is balance.

This is what I would ask you to understand and believe and remember. It is balance that I seek to achieve as I work to heal and restore relationships with civilizations off Earth. I seek to instill a balanced opinion of Earth, neutral and objective.

Myself and my team make note of the ways aspects of life in other cultures are balanced when compared with the even or uneven balance of those same aspects on Earth. We on Earth have a way to go, but I would have us understand the objective from our hearts as well as our minds. We must understand what balance and equality are or we will be working for an unsustainable objective.

Balance is balance. It is not dominance reversed. That applies to every aspect of our relationships amongst ourselves on Earth and to our relationships with the many, many civilizations off Earth as well.

With love and respect,

Quan Yin

MOTHER MARY

Mother Mary's current focus is building a basis for improving relationships through love, compassion and support for mothers and children — all in the context of Oneness.

My Icon

This is my second chance at an icon that I would have to represent me. My first icon drew from a past life that was formative for me. Now, I choose an icon that for me represents where I stand now in relation to the incarnate human family.

The many members of the incarnate human family are to me a beautiful, beautiful garden of growth. My role is to care for that garden, to assist each and every individual who calls upon me, to help them grow, to help them through hard times, to help them celebrate the joyous times. In either there is spiritual growth.

Those who call on me bring me into their lives so that I can in some way help them – through support in times of need, through friendship in times going well and through joy when there are celebrations in their lives. All of these are growth spiritually and can be used as such.

That is the role I will play, helping the growth. That is my joy, my pleasure, my love, my blessing and my friendship – helping people grow.

When Master Teacher Yeshua was training me, Mother Mary frequently worked with him. She often called me stubborn. When I finally asked her how she defined "stubborn," she told me, "Stubbornness is closing your mind and your intuition and your ears and your eyes to the messages we are attempting to use to guide you . . . and persisting when guidance is to cease or change direction."

I discovered that she had high standards for quality and commitment. She did not hesitate to correct me. I soon admired, and then was grateful for the way she could upbraid me if necessary and leave me knowing without a doubt that I was loved. I ended with a genuine "Thank you," for the admonishment.

No one could possibly doubt the love in her heart.

Mother Mary Bio

Current Focus

My focus today? That's building the basis for improved relationships through the love, compassion and support of mothers and children. I would say that is my focus. In carrying this out, in order to build a world where the emphasis can be and is on mothers and children, I focus on relationships at various levels – public relationships, personal relationships and intimate relationships that create the context in which mothers and children operate, in which mothers and children must live. And that would start with the home, the home and the family.

Family leads to community relationships and the relationships of course that spread beyond that and into the world and the Earth of which we are a part. I foster relationships that reflect through each and every person the concept of One, the concept of Oneness. This is where my focus is today.

Favorite or Significant Past Life

I shall pick, rather than most memorable lives. There are many lives known, and many learning lives about family, but my most memorable has to do with the life I had when we were marching through the Sinai, when we had left Egypt and had not yet reached Canaan. That was the most memorable life because it required a deep faith in God, a deep belief in our leader . . . faith in our leader, faith in our heritage, faith in our teachings. It required the utmost of faith, for we built community as we went.

It was also a put-learning-into-practice life where all soul lessons from prior lives had to be drawn in and exercised, drawn in and applied. We needed someone like Zipporah [Moses' wife]. We needed Zipporah and we needed to work with her to keep the families, the mothers, the children cared for. It was a very dynamic time because it was so mobile. It was move and set tentative roots and uproot and move and set tentative roots and uproot and move. I suppose one might consider it similar to those occupations today that require families to pick up and move and pick up and move and pick up and move.

The difference was that when we put down tentative roots, it was not necessarily into an established community that would welcome us, or expected us. So there was much going on in that life, much application of faith and prior-life experiences. And there was much learning – learning to appreciate strength, the strength that is not always gentle, the strength that is not always spoken in the kindest of words, but the strength that is necessary for survival and protection of the mothers and the children so that the entire community will survive.

That would be my most memorable life. Or one of them. I smile. I don't think you expected that.

> *Mother Mary shares her thoughts on the image people have of one another, including our image of her today some 2000 years after the pivotal role she played for humanity.*

Changing One's Image
WeSeekToServe Newsletter, February 2018

Mother Mary

I would like to speak about changing one's image.

This is sometimes very difficult to do, for the image becomes set. And it isn't as if it is just one image. There are many images, all of the same individual. This is perfectly clear in the case of the leader of any country. To those who back the leader, the leader is indeed most welcome, cheered and supported. And for those in opposition, the leader is disliked at minimum, grumbled about or actually vilified. And all of this is a matter of what each individual image is of this country's leader.

My supposition is that the leader is neither so good nor so evil as the avid supporters or the avid detractors would have it.

Now, why do I go into images? I think you will identify with my example. And you will note that, at my request, I am now being called a teacher. My dear friends, I have always been a teacher. From the first time my name appears in Holy Scripture, from the first time any image of me was painted for any meeting place, I have been a teacher. Most especially I love teaching children. I do love our children. There is a love I can say honestly that I would have for every one of you. From that love, I share what I know, I share my experiences and that is my way of teaching. We each teach others in this way because we are all members of the same family.

I would remind you of that. For when your praise is blind of reality and when your vilification is without logical merit, then I would step in and ask you, as your teacher, which position do you think the Lord God takes about this individual? What good is it doing the whole of the human family if everything is perfect or everything is vile about whatever individual you speak of?

You are still one family and I am in the same family you are. And as an elder sister who wishes to teach – from, I might add, lives of imperfection that I remember in my own spiritual journey – please assess with open eyes, open mind and open heart focused on the good of the whole and do not go overboard one way or the other. For it is rare indeed that anyone is so perfect there are no lessons to learn. And it is just as rare that someone is without some wisdom somewhere, somehow or some intention that might have gone very far astray, yet at the core was for the benefit of the whole.

Changing images of yourself and others through love and objective assessment about the needs of the whole, that is what I would ask.

Thank you.

Mary, a mother and a teacher

> *Mother Mary explains why she was chosen for the role we all know and hopes that what she reveals will aid the human family today.*

The Real Message in My Life as Mother Mary

WeSeekToServe.com Open Forum, April 2015

Mother Mary

I would like to speak today about my life as Mother Mary, about the message that was important in that life on Earth.

The message from that life was not that I was the mother of the Hebrew child Yeshua who came to be known to the world as Jesus Christ, but *why* I was chosen as his mother. As it sometimes happens, the real message got lost.

The important message is for you to learn that each of you comes to this world with blank pages in the book of your life, ready to write in it with straight or twisted lines, depending on the life you choose to live. It is the purity of spirit, the honesty of the heart that really matter in a person. And that purity of spirit, that honesty of the heart is the same for every newborn human being.

As you live your life, purity of spirit and honesty of the heart come from having inner peace, from living in God, following the Holy Creator, living in harmony, in peace. These qualities come from living with honor, fulfilling the principles of loving God above all and loving your fellow human beings as you would love yourself, as was transmitted by my son in that lifetime.

It is the purity of the heart and the spirit, the clarity and the light that are important for every soul who incarnates, and to keep these qualities intact throughout your life is very difficult. In that sense, when I was selected before going to Earth for the mission of giving birth to a child whose mission was so vast, those who selected me as his mother paid attention to what was most significant, the qualities of my soul.

It was the qualities that my soul had acquired throughout innumerable incarnations, the light, love and compassion, that made me immaculate, clean, pure and ready for the mission I was entrusted to carry out. And that is the desirable way for each and every human being living on your planet to behave, with purity, a clean heart, love and compassion. It is desirable that you live in peace with yourselves and with each other, that you be respectful of yourself, respectful of diversity, of different beliefs and respectful of each other's land.

That is the life I tried my very best to live. Unfortunately, this message never got through.

Humanity seems determined not to seek the light as a family. Although looking to the light is the easiest thing for souls to do, there are too many places in every village and every nation on Earth where these self-same souls give way to fighting, hatred and vengeance. You are one family and from within this family far too many insist on imposing personal opinions mercilessly, destroying each other, not noticing that this behavior and this destruction could result in the annihilation of the entire family.

Can't you see how easy it is to live for oneself and with oneself within the rules for peace and order, love and harmony? It is true that right now there are areas of the planet where it is almost impossible for people to make these changes all at once. That is why it is so important that, little by little, each person begin to change, become an example for those around them. It is the light which must be contagious, not the darkness.

Unfortunately, the opposite is far too strong these days. The human family is being contaminated with negative energy, from unforgiven family quarrels to mass atrocities on one another. This only brings despair and desperation. Each of these is a dense energy with a very low vibration that builds up around individuals, around groups, around nations ... and around the planet. Now is the time to seek change, before the moment comes when none of Earth's inhabitants will be able to see beyond themselves.

I wish that by all means possible there would begin to be more light, more light in many places around this planet all at the same time. I wish there would be a few more spots, a few more persons, a few more groups who come together and apply all these principles, not only in their meditations but in their daily lives. Then, little by little, with their example and their attitude, the change begins.

I would ask you to be part of that change.

The survival of a spiritual human family through demonstration of a life well-lived is the message of my life as Mother Mary.

It causes me great pain of heart to see what has come of the love that was the guiding principle of my life. It gives me much joy to know that there are those who seek the light and strive to live in the love of the Creator and share that love with all around them through their hearts and their actions.

I am here for those who see me as an intercessor, but I am truly simply one who is further down the spiritual path, one who loves you deeply and will do everything in my power to give you the strength and determination to live your life as I attempted to live mine as Mother Mary.

It is the life you choose to live, the love and light you sow and sustain that will be reflected not only in your own most sacred soul, but in the lives and attitudes of all persons you encounter ... and those you don't encounter as well, because living in love and light is contagious.

I would have you understand the real message in that well-known life and realize that no matter where you are now, you can seek the light, seek purity of heart, and seek to love and respect one another.

That is my only wish.

Mother Mary

> *Mother Mary maintains that everyone has a spiritual basis for living whether they acknowledge it or not. She explains a challenging but important way forward to unify the human family of Earth.*
>
> *Lady Nada, in her article on "Street Fighting and the New Civilization," speaks to the damage that can be fostered on others by those who envision exclusive spiritual franchises. The two articles complement one another.*
>
> *I highly recommend a book by three women who quite unknowingly put Mother Mary's advice into action:* <u>The Faith Club: A Muslim, A Christian, A Jew – Three Women Search for Understanding</u> *by Ranya Idliby, Suzanne Oliver and Priscilla Warner.*

Spiritual Enfranchisement

WeSeekToServe.com Panel Discussion, March 2012

Mother Mary

Enfranchisement is a very tender topic. Because you see, one faith, one school of thought – it does not matter which it is, whether it is in the mainstream or out of the mainstream, whether it is mystic or traditional – there is a magnetism, a magnetism that draws people. And there is, in many instances, a certainty that brings a comfort level, and a touchstone, and what is assumed to be a solid platform upon which they may make their decisions and go through their lives.

Now, this platform may be complete atheism. "There is no Divine Source. There is no Divine Plan. There is no . . . whatever."

So when I speak of spiritual world views, I speak of everyone. Because one way or another, articulated or unarticulated, everyone has a basis, a spiritual basis upon which they build their decisions.

Some may tell you they are not spiritual. I would examine the basis on which they make their decisions about how they think of themselves and how they interact with their fellow citizens, other human beings upon this Earth, and how they interact with their environment. They may clutter the environment and they may stomp on their fellow citizens and they may prune themselves in their mirror and say they do not believe in God. I will not judge them, but I will tell them that they do have a spiritual world view, and their spiritual world view, at this particular point, in this particular incarnation, is that they are the center of the universe and that others do not matter.

I would advise you not to throw stones, because most people, most souls have one, two or several of those lives in their experience.

No matter where you are, I will call the set of values upon which you base your interactions with self, others and environment, your spiritual view.

You may consider yourself to be personally enfranchised. That is fine. The point being that if one group is not talking to another group, if one group decides that their franchise is more valuable – is more ancient, is more this or is less that, more important, more useful – then let them be willing to non-judgmentally share. Let them bring what they feel has value and openly listen to what someone else says, what another group says is the value that they bring.

Unless you, as an incarnate human race, decide that you are going to seek the commonalities and allow for differences branching from that common core, then your chances of finding heaven on Earth diminish. Your chances of finding peace on Earth diminish. Your chances of surviving the shift that is upon us diminish.

However, if and when you, as one human family, decide that you are going to seek the commonalities rather than cling to the defamation of all others, you will find yourselves on the path to spiritual maturity.

We speak of sharing and I would say that too many think of sharing food, they think of sharing their homes, they think of sharing their financial resources, they think of sharing their country's resources. But do they think of sharing their most valued beliefs – be they a conviction that the Divine is in everything, or the conviction that the Divine does not exist?

By sharing I do not mean thundering to say, "My way is the right way!" No. I mean the kind of sharing that one is likely to see after a disaster, where one family that salvages a blanket shares it with another. I speak of sharing that comes from the heart, sharing that comes from the belief that if we do this together, we will all be rather better off than if we each do it independently.

You can have your franchise, your groups can have their franchises, but it is the sharing at the spiritual level that is going to go a very long way in moving humanity forward. Not trying to convert anyone – simply sitting down and sharing until you find the commonalities and can lovingly tease each other about the differences, because you have found the core that binds you into One.

That is what I would say about enfranchisement.

Mother Mary

> *Mother Mary replies to a <u>ThoughtsFromAMaster.com</u> reader.
> The reader and others have found her reply helpful.*

On Prayer

ThoughtsFromAMaster.com Commentary, August 2013

Mother Mary

Reader's Question

I have always wondered and sometimes get confused regarding praying. I do pray often but sometimes I get confused as to whom I am actually praying to or even how to pray. I normally pray for wisdom or guidance. I know we are responsible for our lives and there is no one who going to come down and "fix" our problems. I think it must be more of showing us the way, the direction to head. However, sometimes I'm not really sure on the proper way to pray or who to address. I would really appreciate your input on this.

Mother Mary

I am with you and most happy to respond to this query as there are many, many seekers and light-bearers asking this same question. Most would know more about their soul's purpose in this lifetime, for they sense how crucial "this one" is. They are committed to serve.

You will note that this is entirely different from the "gimme, gimme" type of prayer requesting all types of things – often actual things! – or advantages and advancements for the lower nature. Many if not most such entreaties well, I won't say most but many – are immature requests for temporary ego gratification or for emotional comfort when things are not going exactly as the one doing the praying wills. That person wants to get his or her own narrow way, often creating all kinds of bad karma and by-passing if not fully denying important life lessons and opportunities for spiritual growth.

Prayers of anguish and despair are another matter, for

the "dark night of the soul" passages in life are always registered, those prayers are always heard, always.

You see, it has to do with the quality, and even the quantity of heart in the prayer. This is in part why intent is so much discussed today, but this is not really our topic. Intent can be very self-centered and very self-serving. What is heard is the purity, the sincerity, the heart-feltedness of the prayer, the genuineness of the appeal, which, even though the person may be frightened or very troubled or in pain, involves emotional depth, mental focus and clarity. In other words, presence.

Do you realize how many prayers, desires, even plea bargains go out every day from the billions of inhabitants of this realm? How do you think we cope? Could you possibly imagine?

Luckily, there are cosmic laws in place that handle these myriad issues automatically in many instances. The Law of Karma is one, but it is not the brutal eye-for-an-eye distortion or the "As you sow, so shall you reap" variation based on retribution, retaliation or self-righteousness that you should be associating it with. The Law of Karma is not a law of punishment. It is the greatest of teachers, an opportunity for the soul to progress. Think about that. Think how every crisis in life, and every opening door as well, is an opportunity for wisdom to develop, for progress to ensue as lessons are learned.

You say, dear reader, that you are not always sure about how to pray or who to pray to. The simple answer is, "Pray from your heart, your deepest and highest self, and you will always be heard." That kind of prayer registers above the noise level, as it were.

I would, however, like to mention another facet of praying, one that is newer perhaps but gaining ground. It is actually a science, the science of invocation, whereby you *invoke* our presence, you invite us in to collaboration and connection. At the same time, you *evoke* or call forth in us those qualities and that pull to service that draws us closer by law. There is an opening, an opportunity for co-creation and progress, an opportunity not only for your good or the common good but essentially, in evolutionary terms, for the whole of the race and for all of Mother Earth's creation to advance.

The question of who to pray to is an interesting one. In one sense I would answer, "It does not really matter. It is the soul quality of the prayer that is important." If, however, you have a special relationship with a spiritual guide, guru or saint, or even perhaps a deceased loved one you remain strongly bonded with and trust to guide you, then this quality of love and connection, your faith that you have this connection, can help focus your prayer more keenly, can give it legs, as you say.

I would add one more consideration regarding who or what to pray to and that is the power of – how shall I phrase this? – the power of collective consciousness, the power in numbers. You may have heard of novenas in the Catholic tradition, where certain saints are prayed to over a period of time for certain causes. They have been singled out for help in that particular area and so have an ear for it. I myself have had much, much prayer laid at my feet by women and mothers these many centuries since Palestine.

Then there are the countless souls who have chanted various mantras down the ages. That backdrop becomes massive so that each new one who utters the prayer, who chants the mantra, evokes the amassed power built prayer by prayer by all those who have done the same before. This is especially true about praying out loud.

So, dear reader, there are many "proper" ways to pray. Some groups and individuals have very set prayers, very set customs and rituals of prayer. These too are much practiced and effective, provided as ever, that the heart quality is there.

I invite each and every one to pray in their own fashion. And I invite you, I ask you, to pray for the world. Pray for Mother Earth and help ease her transition by heightening your own vibration, purity and mental clarity while you are praying. Find the still, small place within where dwells your Divine Spark and pray all day through mindfulness, through being present as you go about your duties and activities.

Lastly, I invite you all, dear readers, once again, to invite us into your lives so that we can provide the guidance you so ardently seek, so that we can come closer and inspire your noblest, surest actions in restoring this beautiful planet, in laying the foundations of Oneness and universal collaboration.

My love, my peace, surround you.

Mother Mary

> *Mother Mary uses a metaphor we can all understand to explain the concept of an evolving soul. Lady Nada also spoke on this panel and uses imagery to explain how reincarnation works from inner plane perspectives.*

Soul Evolution

WeSeekToServe.com Panel Discussion, February 2012

Mother Mary

When I think of soul evolution, I think of a child maturing, because that is what souls do. Souls are like children, and sometimes the "advanced souls" are simply those who have benefited from their experiences.

As with children, maturity does not necessarily emerge at a given age. We can have 40-year-old human beings who are not necessarily behaving as responsible adults, but rather acting more child-like. They can be delightful, or they can be annoying. All these terms – child-like, mature, adult – are ways of putting individuals into various categories along the age continuum. We know that these categories exist . . . and we also know of precocious children.

The same can be said for soul evolution.

The human soul continues from life to life to life. If I may say so, Master Yeshua – who many of you would know as Jesus – is one that, in my humble opinion, you could consider a precocious soul. Even when "young," this soul was precocious and matured to express an adult, responsible outlook very quickly.

Other souls are more like – and I smile when I say this, I say this very lovingly – other souls in their personal evolution path are more like the 40-year-old with the child still bubbling forth. Now, children have an advantage in many ways. They can be optimistic, they see no boundaries. That can be desirable, and that can be undesirable. There can be an annoying delight with a 40-year-old who has not lost the ability to view the world as wide-eyed 5-year-old.

Now if the 40-year-old continues to behave like a

rebellious teenager, this could be a little more difficult. But I think you get my point.

This maturing cycle can be the same for souls. Some souls, even though they have lived many lifetimes, will continue to live the same lifetime over and over and over again. This may be likened to the woman who will not let go of the fact that she was once the prom queen, or the man who will not give up the fact that in high school he was the basketball star.

Souls can express similar attachments, but their attachment is to past lives rather than past events in a single life. These souls may *intend* to move past this image when they incarnate. Yet free will comes with every incarnation. When they actually manifest on the physical plane, they simply continue, for the most part, to live out the life that they had when they were an influential, upper class, wealthy individual, for whatever time it was in.

Maybe they were heading a local business group. Or maybe they were a mother superior in the convent, or they were married to the prince of the realm and became a princess through marriage, or they were the king, etc. Reliving the past can be a pattern that hinders the maturing of souls just as it hinders the maturing of an incarnated individual.

Now obviously, with a human incarnation there is a birth and a death. With souls it is not quite the same. Souls come into existence – which is a totally different process that we are not going to go into here – and souls eventually mature to such a degree that their vibrations, their light, the light of their maturity, is indistinguishable from the light of the maturity of the Divine, the Creator of our Cosmos and beyond. In that way, one could call it ceasing to exist as an individual soul, because the vibrations are indistinguishable from the Divine.

Yet at any point, when they have reached that Divine level of maturity, they can remember every instance in their life from "childhood" to "full maturity." It is being able to remember each and every single life. So there is a continuity, a continuation of individual memories, but those individual memories have been contributed to the total memory of the Divine.

Individual memories can be separated, yet they contribute to the totality of the Divine, just as the memory of a specific year in your life, or even a specific event, contributes to the totality or who you are today.

Maybe you won a prize for art or singing or leadership when you were in school, or your family gave you a very special birthday party when you turned 13. As a full grown adult with grandchildren, you will still remember that special party, remember that special day when maybe a younger brother or sister was introduced into the family.

Just as you can remember those special days no matter how old you get, when you reunite with the Divine to such a degree that your vibrations are indistinguishable, you can still remember the individual lives.

The full explanation of living life after life after life, I will leave to Master Kuthumi. I bow to Master Kuthumi on that issue[1]. But you see the pattern.

It has been said "as above, so below," and one can see this in the evolution of the soul from life to life to life just as one can see this in what I shall call the evolution, or maturing, of an individual human being in an individual incarnation.

That would be my perspective on the evolution of the soul. This process can be phrased and have a very technical explanation within our realm, the spirit realm of Creation. But make it simple. Think of the people you know, the instances in your own life, and realize that the maturing of a soul is the same pattern at a much different and broader scale of manifestation.

I thank you.

Mother Mary

---

[1] In *Reincarnation – Earth and Elsewhere*, volume 3 of the *Ageless Wisdom Evolving* series, Master Teacher Kuthumi explains the evolution of the reincarnation process on Earth. The process on other planets differs. Omstara is one of the Off-Earth Allies who explain how the reincarnation process works on their home world.

> *Under some conditions, Mother Mary asks to be addressed as "Mary." Her colleagues in the Community, for example, all call her simply "Mary." Sometimes she signs her messages "Mary." This is one of those times. This message is Mary clearly in her role as a Master Teacher from the Community of Spiritual Masters.*

All We Ask Is That You Listen
WeSeekToServe.com Open Forum, October 2014

Mother Mary

I am Mary. I would have a message to the readers of WeSeekToServe.

There has been a great deal said about the shift and about the world today. These things are being said by two different groups of people. I will call the first group the spiritually aware people who are expecting to be led to a new dimension, a new world that does not have the downside of including the portion of the human population that is not so spiritually aware.

I would like to make it perfectly clear that this is not the case. The human family <u>*will not be split.*</u> This is important to remember and to realize. What happens to one happens to all.

What we need is to unite the human family. Unite them in love, in respect, in adherence to some basic laws of reality in living together on one planet.

We from the Community of Masters have been saying for several years now that the goal of the human family is Oneness. We have been saying that the energies that bind the human family together cannot be disbanded and go away at your convenience. This means that one group cannot start slaughtering another group and call it justified. This cannot be. One group cannot impose their will and supposed superiority on another group and call it justified.

It is time that the human family of Earth begins to understand and practice the ramifications of being One. This must be done. There is no other choice if humanity is to move forward.

Unity must be established and that established unity must flow through the cities of the world, through the refugee camps of the world, through the landscape and jungles and forests and river deltas of this world. The unity must be made to exist because the human family of Earth chooses, of free will, to begin to live in unity.

Today, we have a great chaos upon this planet. We, from our perspective, see how damaging this chaos is and see how far it can spread. Why then, is it so difficult for the second group, the political and economic and religious leaders of this world, to realize that they have a significant role to play in relieving the human family of this chaos? Why? We do not understand.

From our perspective, the perspective of those who love humanity but are in a position where all we can do is sit and watch, we would welcome an invitation to come and discuss the possibilities for moving forward to a better, more equal world. A world of equal opportunity for spiritual fulfillment for all, a world where no one imposes beliefs on another. We would have the violence against other human beings be put to an end. This we would have.

Where is the band of leaders who will acknowledge our existence and listen to what it is we have to say? That is our question. One way or another, we, on our side, have worked with human beings for some time. We have had meetings, we have had teachings. Yet we are not on the invitation list when conferences are held about dealing with the violence, the oppression and the slaughter that ensues day after day.

We are here.

We are able to assist with our guidance and our experience. If you would, we have maps that will give you options for extricating yourselves from the impenetrable forest of hate and violence. The maps are free, but they are not necessarily easy to follow. The cost of extricating yourselves is steep because you have become so deeply entrenched in the attitudes of war. But these maps do exist and we offer them for free. All you need do is ask and listen with open ears.

Please be willing to gather, you who make the decisions about war, about oppression of other human beings, you who cry for peace and freedom. We are ready to share our perspectives and our experience.

With hope and blessing,

Mary

> *Cosmic Law prevents members of the Community of Masters from interfering with the actions or decisions of the incarnate human family. However, the Community can and does respond to requests.*

We Come By Request Only

WeSeekToServe.com Panel Discussion, January 2016

Mother Mary

We are looking this month at the effects of shifting your point of view and asking for help. But this must be asking for help, I would say, from the most useful frame of mind. And who is it who must ask for help? That is the next question and I would like to address both.

Asking for help from the most effective frame of mind is looking inward and upward to the greater good of the whole and asking for guidance for the greater good of the entire human family. This can be very difficult when you have a particular problem right on your doorstep. This can be very difficult when you are concerned, desperately concerned for those you love, be they near or far, those you care about, those you would have safe from danger and the chaos that consumes the human family today.

But the most effective frame of mind to ask for help is indeed to look inward to your inner guidance that is ever in the light if you take a deep breath and realize that your heart is a direct connect to your soul and your soul has a connect to the Lord God. And look upward, look upward to the angels. Look upward to those you would consider saints.

And if you do not believe in angels and saints, look upward to those who have passed on and have a broader perspective than you do, those who have achieved wisdom, those who no longer need to come to Earth to incarnate, those from the Masters of Wisdom who live in the Community of Masters. Look upward and ask for help. You can look upward and ask for aid from the Off-Earth Allies who have a vast array of experience.

When your pleas for assistance, when your concern is

for the whole, for the greater good of the human family, you are asking for help from the light, and those pleas will always be heard. And the more we hear, the easier it is to respond.

The next thing I would speak of is who it is who must ask, for clearly, any one and every one of you can ask for support and assistance, can ask for guidance, can ask for insights. Who most needs to shift perspective and ask? And send the request upward to those who are further down the spiritual path? Who must do that most?

Well, it is those who can benefit most from being answered, from receiving the aid they request. Who are they? At this point, we would say from our perspective that it is the decision-makers who walk the Earth among you, those who are decision-makers within the shifting populations and those who are decision-makers at the highest political, social and economic status in the world communities.

It is these decision-makers we would reach if at all possible and encourage them with our outreach of love and light so they realize that once they have shifted their perspective, keeping their focus on the high energies, the high frequencies of greater good for all, we will be able to respond to them. And if enough of them issue the request for assistance in the context of the greater good, then we will be better able to act and respond.

I would like to take a moment to consider what that response might be, what it might look like. That response might be a dream that gives them a new perspective. It might be a flash of insight that they never expected. It might be an "accidental" meeting. It might be an unexpected visit from someone with a fresh and new idea. These are some of the ways we will respond.

We will provide guidance, advice. We can give a lot of advice in dreams to those who dream and remember their dreams. This can be the response. But ever the perspective and the context of the request come from looking inward to your spiritual core, looking upward to those further down the path, or both.

Please remember this in your own life, with your own problems. As close as those problems are, pray for the greater good, for the greater good of the whole and this will be humanity's path forward to calm the chaos: ever higher frequencies, ever the light, ever the greater good. This is where the strength of the human family will lie.

I thank you very much. I wish you well and I hope that you remember my words.

With love,

Mother Mary

> *A WeSeekToServe reader asked the Master Teachers to speak to the existence of so many different gods.*
> *Quan Yin and Lady Nada also spoke on this panel.*

Many Traditions – Many Gods

WeSeekToServe.com Panel Discussion, May 2012

Mother Mary

Are these gods real? The gods that people turn to, the gods that they ask for help, the gods they seek blessings from, the gods that they placate with their offerings, with sacrifices in their lives, with respect that they give, with obedience to rules they have been told exist about the proper relationship with this god or that god or all gods?

We spoke, a while back, of spiritual enfranchisement, of finding the core truths that exist for humanity and humanity's spiritual growth – spiritual growth defined as achieving a civilization that recognizes and supports the Oneness of all. I think I will use that as a simple definition. And we, of the Spiritual Hierarchy, are going to be coming forth to walk among you. That we covered last month. We are coming forth now, we will be coming forth as a team, as a unit, as advisors.

Now, what does this mean to the religious practices of those who put their faith in these multifarious gods?

I would say some of these gods are beings of power who came forth, each in their own time, each in their own way, and they brought messages. They brought Divine love. Now, I cannot account for the individual behaviors and philosophies of every deity in every culture since time began. But they do have in common their relationship to humanity, and that is, one way or another, a power that human beings do not have. That, in my mind, is what makes them godlike. They have abilities, they have power "ordinary human beings" do not have.

And I would say the one missing word is "yet." They have wisdom and power that ordinary humanity does not possess *yet*.

If one counts perfection as Divinity, I think you will find

that many of these gods were not perfect in all regards, especially if they had temper tantrums and lost their temper with humanity. So were they perfect? No, I don't think so, unless one is redefining the word perfection.

Did they have a function and a purpose? I would say, yes. They can be very specialized. But I would ask you what specialty, what moral characteristics, any of these divine beings has that human beings, at some point, do not have.

The power of compassion, the power of being willing to sacrifice themselves, the power of loving enough to say, yes, I will protect your newborn child. Yes, I will bless the seeds you plant in this crop so that you may provide for yourself and your family. Yes, I will bless your journey so that you arrive safely.

Do not human beings, one from another, have these same powers? Cannot a community and medical practice and alternative healing all protect a newborn? If you protect the mother and protect the child and make certain that the mother has been treated well during pregnancy and has had sufficient nutrition and has not had to labor beyond her capacity, and you make certain that the child is born in a clean and sanitary way, and treated with love welcomed into the world, cannot a community and human functions provide for the welfare and health of this child? I would say yes.

Can human beings bless one another? Yes, they can bless with the love in their heart. Can human beings aid one another? Yes, they can. If a child is lost, or a spouse is lost or a parent dies, cannot people aid one another to sustain those who are so terribly hard hit with grief?

There is a certain amount of comfort that comes from thinking that there are powers beyond humanity to do these functions. But you see, these functions are inside. These functions come with a human vehicle – if you find them within, and if you touch what the soul intended when it came into this incarnation, and understand where your place is in relation to those who are further along the road and to those who are not so advanced.

I would caution. The one place where I would question "gods" is in angry vengeance. There are consequences for actions and there are consequences for decisions. There are always consequences, but true Divinity does not practice angry vengeance. One must understand consequences, but this can be done in a loving forgiving, manner, in which the objective is the opportunity to balance and learn lessons of balance.

When we of the Spiritual Hierarchy come forth to walk among you, we will bring wisdom, we will bring our advice, we will bring our powers, such as they are. But we guide and advise and assist, we covered that last time. Nothing has changed.

For all our wisdom and all our power, we are not gods. We are simply further along. And many of those who have come in the past with messages vital to humanity's spiritual growth are left with the legend of the Divine, when they were volunteer messengers. Not angels, messengers who cared about their brethren and wished to show the next step in human spiritual maturity.

They became gods because their legend is empowered. What is needed to be seen is that they were simply in a place of evolution where all human beings will be at one point.

See a path stretching, here to there, A to Zed. Human beings, human souls are intended to travel that path, *are* traveling that path, and at the end is reunification with the Divine. When these beings and these energies called gods can be recognized as beings and energies and powers and skills and compassion that is being demonstrated by an individual who is further down the path, humanity will take a long step toward spiritual maturity. They will take a step toward respecting the extent of the Divine creativity *within*, the soul's creative heart, the creativity expressed so many ways already – especially in finding ways to help each other.

This creativity is one of humanity's strengths. But unless that creativity is turned to help partner with Mother Earth, unless it is turned to help one another create an environment that is safe for everyone, an environment where every soul can incarnate and find its own path, a creativity that protects family and those you love, a creativity that realizes "those you love" are far, far more multifarious than you might imagine, then you have not yet recognized and tapped the Divine creativity within.

Many of these gods and energies are simply demonstrations of what human beings can do for each other.

When you reach the point where you cannot carry on because you are simply too drained, you can look for help inside with your soul and touch your soul, perhaps, and find a peace there, because your soul is a spark of God. Or you can look to your friends and neighbors who will rally round you, and you will find that you are sustained because they are expressing Divinity in the way they help care for you.

Or you can send your prayers to those who are further down the road and say with your powers, "Please help me figure this out." We will listen and assist in such ways as we are able, but we are not gods.

We are simply further down the road, reaching back to help. And that is an important distinction, because being further down the road is letting you know that one day you will be where we are, and perhaps you will remember to reach back.

You can start practicing today, and in many instances – in many, many instances – this kind of practice is seen around the world. Reaching out, reaching back to help one another. Is this not what gods do?

Thank you,

Mother Mary

> *Mother Mary feels strongly about the human family evolving as one, unified whole. Rapid evolution of consciousness is necessary to keep pace with Earth's vibrational shift as well as to speed the human family's return to Source.*

Facing the Challenge of Expanding Consciousness – Part 1

WeSeekToServe.com Panel Discussion, January 2015

Mother Mary

I first wish to outline what it means for humanity to expand consciousness whether it is in a group or as an individual. Enriching consciousness is essentially the purpose of human evolution on this planet. It is expanding one's awareness and lifting it to a higher plane where it is possible to understand all that surrounds the individual as a soul in evolution.

Awareness begins with understanding oneself in the physical and then proceeds on a trajectory of expanding into realms that cannot be perceived by the five textbook senses. It is easy to begin by visualizing what surrounds you in the dense physical world. It is not so easy for the bulk of humanity to see the etheric or realm of spirit that surrounds the dense physical body, although this sight is becoming more and more utilized by those incarnate, and means of photography to capture the etheric have been developed. Thus, consciousness expands.

The realm of spirit surrounds each and every one of you. Spirit is what we all are essentially – you on your side of the veil and we on our side. For a fuller understanding of yourselves as incarnate beings whose bodies extend beyond the dense physical, you must venture into the realm we call spirit. This you do individually and in groups.

I cannot fully enough express the importance of this topic at this critical time on planet Earth. You have heard from many sources that the energies of Earth are shifting rapidly and as I explained in my Open Forum article of October 2014, "All We Ask Is That You Listen," the human family will not be split.

All rise or all stumble. To rise together and keep pace with the planet means expanding your awareness of who you are beyond the physical presence you see before yourselves.

Having said this, let me also explain that it is fully necessary to realize that none of you is truly alone in this world. You are in truth a collection of human souls all interfacing and interacting with each other without completely understanding that you are essentially brother-sister souls in total unity. You are one family. Your work therefore is always in unity with the rest of humanity. Individually you progress, yes, but collectively you are moving forward as a single family unit rather than as individuals separated by time and space.

What you achieve as individuals is what you achieve for all. Your individual progress affects the entire human family. There is no escaping from this fact. Thus, collectively though invisible to your outward perceptions, you are connected with one another as nodes in a massive energy network.

You may ask, "How can we even begin to quickly expand all human consciousness and effectively change the way we live on this planet?" There is no secret to this: the information has been given out even in the most ancient times in texts and teachings on how the human family relates to Source, to the Creator, to God, even if those were not the exact terms used.

If you wish to speak in terms of your relationship with God, in fact you are speaking of your group goal, of closing the gap between incarnating humanity and your spiritual Source, of realizing spiritual unity with the Creator that so many call God. How can there be anything more joyous than this ultimate unity?

The human family has always been loved and guided from above. Spirit is always beckoning humanity home to your rightful place in this huge universe. Nothing can prevent this reunification with your spiritual source.

For too long the family of Earth has lived in darkness and with much despair. The human family has lived in ignorance of the fact that, in unity, they are truly the sons and daughters of the same Creator. As you begin to recognize that you are on the path of return to your true home in the heavens or however you may see it, you begin to become more and more excited about this possible reunion with Source.

The family of Earth is at a point in human history when I believe the doors are now open wider than ever before for the entire family to find the portals that will lead quickly into a new way of living. This new way of living is essentially knowing that you are a spark of the God that many pray to, but you have forgotten this fact. It is only by recognizing this fact in yourself and all your brothers and sisters in the same human family that together you can reach this goal of returning home quickly and more easily than you could ever have previously imagined.

Now is the hour of quickening your pace. Recognize that you are not alone but rather evolve and grow with your brother-sister souls. The quicker you can find common cause to work together, the sooner you will discover that your path will be paved with wonderful surprises. Your journey will be without divisions or separatist ways, without anger or hatreds, without all those thoughts and emotions that would slow or block your swift passage home.

When human consciousness expands enough to recognize the unity of humankind, there will be few hindrances to achieve great progress in all things.

There is yet much that humanity can do to create a physical world that will support a better quality of life for all. On this planet you can create a world where none suffer from hunger, disease or want, from anything that would hinder passage on the path home. Only your own actions can block your return. We spiritual guides know well that it is only you who can slow your return. This results from the inability to see clearly that disunity amongst yourselves as incarnate human beings, not disunity among your souls, is the ultimate cause of your pain and suffering. There is therefore absolutely no reason for anyone to be suffering from want or suffering from lack of awareness of who they are in this greater universe.

Look inward, look outward, look to your own spiritual wisdom and see clearly that you and the entire universe are One. If this is true – and I know that it is – then you have no reason to perpetuate separation within your own worldwide, human family.

I have been fully dedicated to assisting humanity in any

way within the cosmic laws that exist. I cannot disobey the laws in my relationship to the human family of Earth. What I can do is encourage you to trust me and trust that I seek to protect you within what the laws permit. I come to teach you what I can within the law.

I ask you to come to me because there are no laws that prevent you from seeking me and those in the spiritual kingdom with whom I work. Nothing stands in your way. I am here as are many others who seek to assist Earth's human family and expand your consciousness as quickly as possible.

Know that you are loved and guided always.

Mother Mary

> *Mother Mary presents a strong case for self-love, love of others and love of the whole being inextricably intertwined.*
> *Lady Nada was also on this panel and speaks of the love that exists between two souls.*

Together We Love

WeSeekToServe.com Panel Discussion, November 2013

Mother Mary

My colleagues have covered much on the topic of love and as you know, historically, much has been imputed to me in this domain as the Mother, an exponent of motherly love. And this is a role I continue to nourish, to stand behind. But I would have you look at it from my perspective – in terms of one of the greatest needs, contemporary needs, in this domain. And that is the need for each and every one of you to *love yourself*.

Yes, to love yourself. You are spiritual beings. Your souls are sparks of God.

You have been taught down the ages to love others, to do unto others, etc., etc., in terms of the Golden Rule. And this is of course very good advice. However, you must also, if not first, love yourself. For in loving yourself, you will know how to love others and automatically render that love you deeply feel – and feeling is the operative – as well as knowing yourself and others. At the deepest level, they are one and the same. But in contemporary society, there is a dearth, a great, great lack of self-love. So many of you are turned outward, are looking outward ever for love, approval, connection, and yet do not really know and therefore cannot really love yourselves, or vice versa, cannot truly love and then know yourselves.

So much of societal action, education and focus in the developed world is harshly controlled by perfectionistic standards. These standards are not only unattainable, they sap the life force, the creativity, the capacity to love and be loved in so many ways ... leading to isolation and self-loathing, self-neglect and even many forms of self-mutilation. I would mention the obsession over dieting, for example, and some of the "modern" diseases of self-absorption like obesity, anorexia, bulimia, etc. that occur not only as concerns food but in many other arenas as well. They are most fundamentally a neglect of self, a lack of loving oneself.

The many forms of this lacking stir my motherly heart and the hearts of all those on this side of the veil who would gladly partner with you, support you, love you back, approve of you if you could only unlock the gates to your own hearts, self-knowledge and self-acceptance. There is a great starvation in the developed world.

And then in so many other areas of the world there is strife and chaos and fear – much fear – and teeming masses. People in yet other areas are falling amid incomprehensible warfare and animosity, living in places where there is no peace. People in abject fear, literally in survival mode, people fleeing for their lives ... all of this is another heart-breaking consequence of heartlessness and lack of brotherly love.

So I would have you find that key to loving yourselves and to loving others and to act like the brothers and sisters of the human family that you are, laying down your arms, your competition, your greed, your neediness, and finding your love of self and your brotherhood/sisterhood in the one human family. When you do this, when you find this love and begin to express it creatively in sharing, it generates both self-respect and the respect of the other, and the respect for the One.

This respect shows you the way, allows you to operate at a different level. And every bit of self-love and self-respect that you generate influences all around you such that a great tide of love could quickly occur in the world, replacing the great cry of anguish that is currently clamoring, clamoring throughout Mother Earth and reaching far beyond like a scream. And every bit of love, self-love and love for the other opens a pathway to us as well, those among the Community of Spiritual Masters and your spiritual allies, your Off-Earth Allies and your Deva Allies, who are doing what they can but would have an open door to partner with you and could do so much more.

Take a moment every day to go within ... follow the breadcrumbs, find your inner self, your love for self and your inner peace. And finding that, loving yourself, you can contribute at the most fundamental, the deepest level, to saving the world, this world, now.

    With all my love,

    Mary

> *Mother Mary paints quick portraits of the world today, the world to come and the uncertainty of transition between the two. She reminds us that our elder brothers and sisters are there to work with us as a new civilization begins to emerge.*
>
> *One year later, in the next article, "Planting the Seeds of the New Earth," Mother Mary returns to the New World theme with an even more sanguine outlook.*
>
> *Omstara also spoke on the "Working Together" panel.*

Working Together

WeSeekToServe.com Panel Discussion, April 2016

Mother Mary

My dear children:

My colleagues have said much about the perilous transition you have entered as Earth shifts frequency and a new world emerges, and about the gifts that we, your guides and allies, have to offer in easing your path. They have spoken of our upmost desire to be by your side and assist you through the shoals.

May I suggest that what is most needed for this to occur at this time is quite simply a change in the collective heart of humanity.

A change of heart so that you recognize that you are not alone, that separation is an illusion, that you are One Human Family which is part of a much larger family that loves and cherishes you.

A change of heart as well, whereby you fully realize that your current political and economic structures, no matter how intricately entrenched, are corrupt, are obsolete and serve no one, not even the privileged few who now tremble at the precariousness of their privilege or shoulder on complacent or oblivious of the karma they are heaping on their own backs.

A change of heart whereby you can simply allow for the possibility that your fate is not sealed under these controls, that you can rise above the drudgery, the despair and the utter exhaustion that so many of you are experiencing now. This is occurring now because you are sensitive beings caught in the death throes of the current civilization. But deep in the human heart is much of resiliency. When you allow for the possibility, when you but glimpse, you will realize that you can escape all this and live in dignity.

Can you allow for the possibility? Will you open your hearts to the hope and trust that what we are telling you is true, that our help is yours to seize and command?

Imagine living in dignity, each and every one, as a beloved child of God, whatever name you ascribe. Imagine greeting the day knowing that you have been heard from above and that you count – that whatever you are freely doing to build the new world makes a difference and will be leveraged one hundred fold. You have all the tools and ingenuity required. Together as brothers and sisters you can marshal the will to get it rolling.

A new world is forming in the wings, on the horizon, underground. Despite all appearances, many are the green shoots now rising of justice and rightful sharing. Be not distraught.

I ask, dear reader, that you look deep into your own heart. What is it you would like to contribute? What is your deepest longing for the new time?

With love and wisdom, we await your answer. We stand knocking at the door that only you can answer. Greet us, your loving elders come to serve, and consider now what role you can play in this great awakening.

Your loving Mother Mary

> *Mother Mary returns to the theme of transition to the New Earth that she began a year earlier in the previous article, "Working Together."*
>
> *Lady Nada also spoke on this panel.*

Planting the Seeds of the New Earth

WeSeekToServe.com Panel Discussion, Spring 2017

Mother Mary

My dear lightworkers – those who already are, those who are becoming lightworkers and those who will be – it is time to unite your efforts with ours, making the most of the increasing vibration of your world, which makes it easier for us to collaborate with you. It is time to work as a team, you and us. This increase in vibration on your plane allows us to reach a better communication with you. It also favors a desire for change, a desire to move – it favors action.

To use an analogy, you get the land ready and plant some seeds, then we come after you and we plant other seeds, different ones, seeds we know can help you to change. We have planted some already and are planting many more. We will water these seeds with vibrations of love, with vibrations of hope and of knowledge, and we will be patient. We are waiting and will wait to see how these seeds, planted with love and watered with love and light, tended sometimes at great sacrifice, begin to sprout and produce those green shoots Master Morya was speaking about some time ago (WeSeekToServe.com Open Forum, June 2015) and mentions again in his message in this issue.

Those sprouts of change will break through the Earth's crust, the crust of darkness, and will foster change. They will give you the strength, the courage, the energy, the clarity of vision and better criteria to begin making the changes needed to achieve that New Earth, that better world, that more fulfilling and complete life ... starting as newly-born plants that shoot out of the earth with strong stems. With time and patience we will have a marvelous crop of strong plants, of nourishment for the soul, nourishment for the greater human family.

So here we are, all of us working side by side to manage to save humanity and achieve unification in the human family. The human family is beginning to unify to achieve this objective. All of you in different parts of the planet, in different ways, each in your own way, all of you are beginning to collaborate with your personal change and with the change in what surrounds you. You are beginning to work in the plantation so to speak, on that crop that we wish to be rich and grow full of wonderful fruits.

This has been done on other planets, and it has been done on planet Earth at some moments of its history – exceptional moments that fostered a change, a shift in the evolution of humanity in previous times. Those changes, those shifts, somewhat abrupt and surprising or unexpected, have been favored by us in cooperation with you, with souls that have incarnated in each such lifetime to foster those changes. And that is also happening nowadays, in a different way for we are in an era of rapid communications, of social media, of speed in everything, in knowledge, in the transmission of news and events and where everything, even the smallest thing, gets magnified, be it good or bad. We need to focus this work now in this way for that will yield great results.

That is why we have the hope that the good things, the good seeds magnify and propagate and that they rapidly reach from one end to the other of the planet so that the changes can take place faster than at other times of your history.

Therefore be prepared for rapid changes. Know that everything responds to a plan for the salvation and unification of the human family, to a plan made with love.

With love, I bid you farewell.

My blessings,

Mother Mary

> *Mother Mary's year-end advice: there is more to clear at year end than the rooms. Clear it all!*

Mother Mary's Year-End Message
WeSeekToServe Newsletter, December 2018

Mother Mary

Dear ones:

There is a saying that translates more or less into a multitude of languages that I would point out at this pivotal time of year and of history: "Clean the room, welcome the guest."

"Clean the room" being so appropriate in so many ways. Do you not relate? So much stuck energy ... It may be neglected piles and corners in your house that need clearing, stale ideas cluttering up your mind, lives you have outlived that need to be packed away so you can move on to the next chapter, even just "stuff" that could happily be serving others if you just let it go.

How much just needs to be cleared forgiveness-wise too, so that you can start the new year with a clean, clear slate, shoulders unburdened.

Now is the time, now is the moment to divest yourselves of all that is weighing you down from the past and all that you can pass on for others to give new life to and use. Let it all go. Activate those channels, part with what you can pass on and bury the rest.

And keep your eyes open, for that spirit of new openness and sharing happens on all levels – whatever you need will come your way too. Everyone gets to feel lucky where there is clearing and movement. Everyone gets to feel blessed in a special way. I can say this to you, I who once felt taken care of by the warmth and comfort of clean hay as my time drew near.

Call upon me, Mary, your heavenly mother, but also on my colleagues, depending on your ancestry and circumstances. Call upon us, Quan Yin, Isis, Ninsun, Gaia and all, for we support you always. Know that your prayer is a connection, an opening for grace to flow toward and enfold you whenever you need enfolding, but also now, as the old year wanes and the new one glimmers, now and ever.

May you welcome the guest – many guests – in the year to come. Make haste to clean the room, to open the space in your hearts and minds, to help bring much-needed light and clearing into this world.

Your loving mother,

Mary

OMSTARA

Omstara comes from Cygnus. Her work here is balancing energies. She assists the Community in building progressive movements.

(Color is Gold)

My Icon

I would say my icon is adequate. It has all the elements I wanted plus it gives an image of richness and abundance and light, which all bring joy to people, and gold is always positive to the eye. Besides, it's the color of divinity. Those colors suit my mission.

Once trained, I did a fair amount of work with the devas in their etheric kingdom. (Devas and Angels are technically in the same kingdom, but their responsibilities are quite different. Angels guide and protect. Devas design and build just about everything attributed to Mother Nature.)

I was working with several devas in a flowered patch to one side of a pathway. We spotted a tall, graceful woman in a long, white gown walking with some of the senior devas. She had an aura of dignity about her. When the party reached our small work group, she stopped and commented on the human among them and asked about me. My friends looked at me, so I answered her.

"You can hear me?" she said.

"Yes," I answered.

At that she smiled, introduced herself and spelled her name. "I think we'll be working together one day," she said as her party moved on.

Her prediction proved to be accurate.

I especially enjoy the variety of exercises that Omstara suggests in her teachings.

Omstara Bio

Current Focus

I am here to work and cooperate with the Community of Masters. My main feature is working with the energy of joy. I try to bring joy to every situation in which I work. I try to teach how to reach the energy of joy. When we who are working to help humanity to raise its vibration work on how to spread and instill the energy of joy, we are counteracting the darkness, and in the blending of all these energies, something better comes out which tends to be harmonious.

Harmony comes from the mixture of joy about where you are living, of how and what you are experiencing and the acceptance of all of it. That doesn't mean that if your life is terrible you do not try to improve it, of course. But the energy of joy will give you a push if such is the case to try and come out of it, and especially to avoid that your entire soul's energy be contaminated by rage, resentment, hatred or fear. These states can exist, but they are mixed and counteracted by joy.

So that is my work with the Community at this time on Earth, spreading joy, teaching joy, taking joy everywhere it is needed. I also enjoy people who are joyful because their joy nourishes me as well and their joy spreads and "contaminates" all around them. It's kind of contagious!

I have been here on Earth for a long time now but there were many lives that I spent somewhere else, on other planets doing the same job and learning as well. Learning how to create, spread and contaminate with joy. However, I was on planet Earth many, many lifetimes ago in the time of Atlantis and later in Egypt. It is with great pleasure that I come now to help humanity to raise its frequency.

My Favorite or Significant Life

You asked me about a favorite past life. I very much enjoyed the years, the lifetimes I spent learning in other dimensions how to handle, how to create and how to work with joy. I was a privileged being, having been chosen to do this learning and have this task later on – the task of spreading joy.

Thank you, that is all.

> *Omstara builds on "What goes around, comes around." Her perspective sounds simple. Yet it can be quite an informative experience to apply her remarks to a review of one's recent behavior and decisions, rather like the thought experiments scientists engage in.*

Adventures in Spiritual Growth

WeSeekToServe.com Panel Discussion, June 2014

Omstara

One can begin to understand their purpose in life when they take the time to dwell upon certain concepts of life, whether about themselves or about others.

Life lessons can be quite hard to take at times, difficult to endure and difficult to remember, difficult to live through, difficult to see through ... but they are all part of the journey that each person must live. How that person decides to see life, to observe, to register and make decisions based on their experience is when it can range from being fun to being miserable, being an adventure or something unsurmountable that crushes the spirit. Each person must choose their stance, and each must bear the consequences.

We try to encourage the citizens of Earth to consider that each action they take is a building block to their next days of existence. An uplifted heart will bring uplifted days in the future and vice-versa. We see so many outcomes.

Human beings often feel powerless in the face of what befalls them, but this is where they have the most power ... and that power comes in the form of thought-building. The attitude you take and the thoughts that follow will be the very steps that lead you down, or up, or forward. Those very thoughts will lead you to a selection of doors to walk through on the adventure of your spiritual growth.

For example, should you make the decision to retaliate against someone who has harmed you personally through spite, then you are likely mirroring the same spiteful attitude that person approached you with. You have returned this hurt and thus it will be returned to you. That is one possible adventure.

Another possible adventure would be to understand as best you can the reason for this person's behavior and chose not to mirror it. That adventure will take you in the opposite direction and lead you to further, quite different adventures. This is not difficult to understand – it simple takes a moment to foresee and calculate which adventure you wish to experience.

Some choices open doors while some close doors. It is important to understand that a closed door is its own kind of adventure. Nonetheless, choosing to view your life as an adventure can be quite uplifting and can guide your thoughts towards making those choices that give you the adventures best suited to your spiritual growth.

Listen to your heart for guidance. Understand that difficulty is sometimes exactly the measure needed to produce moments of conscious expansion. Take note and experiment with observing the outcomes of your actions with purposeful intent. Your perceptions will surely change and filter in the difference. You need not hold the world on your shoulders when it is far better to open your experience to the whole world and allow your spiritual perception to advance your view.

Thank you,

Omstara
(from the constellation Cygnus)

> *Omstara speaks of the technical steps necessary before the human family and the Ascended Master Teachers can begin collaborating and can begin truly working together.*
> *Mother Mary also spoke on this panel.*

Working Together

WeSeekToServe.com Panel Discussion, April 2016

Omstara

My colleagues and I have been insisting on the need to have you, as members of the human family, request our help and presence so that we can, within our laws, assist and collaborate with you. We suppose that many of you will be asking yourselves: How can this collaboration take place? How can these beings from other dimensions be able to reach us?

Well, here is the answer: an increase in the vibrational frequency of each and every person in the human family brings as a result an increase in the vibration of the family as a whole. This allows you to reach other realms where the vibration is more subtle, and it is in those realms that we dwell. It will be the similarity of the vibration between the human family and ours that will foster and make it easier for us to share all that we can offer for your evolution and progress.

We on our side are doing our part of the work making it possible for us to descend to denser vibrations and therefore get closer to the vibration of incarnate humans on Earth. It remains for all of you to work on increasing your own vibrations to bring them closer to ours. There is a thin veil that separates us from you but it is not insurmountable and all our efforts and yours must be directed to unifying those vibrations.

How can each person contribute to raising the vibration of the human family? Well, evidently it is an individual job as we have already said. It is the sum of many individual efforts, of all the individual work, that is going to raise the energy of the planet. If each one of you has the awareness of what you are – that is, spiritual beings of light and vibration – if each of you is aware of your soul, of your Higher Self, and works on improving the vibration and the communication with that Higher Self; if each one of you watches your own attitudes, your behavior towards others; if each person strengthens the love within themselves, their self-love and self-esteem; if each person improves their love towards others, their fellow human beings, the sharing and the empathy; if you practice gratefulness ... all of this would bring an immense joy to the human race and contribute to raising each family member's soul vibration.

As the family vibration rises, each person will be more capable of perceiving the subtle realms where we dwell and will be able to receive personalized information to improve themselves and move forward ... and consequently to improve, move forward and heal the problems and chaos existing on Earth. Thus it is one person's individual work plus another individual's work, plus that of another and another ... the sum of many individual works, and later on the work of groups, that will make the rise in vibration so great that it will make it possible to communicate with us. We look forward to this.

Every day, more and more people in the human family are working on this goal, more and more groups are gaining the awareness that the only way to progress is by living in a different way, feeling differently, experiencing joy and happiness, living in peace, justice, equity and sharing.

That change in behavior means having the awareness that you are One Family where all of you are siblings, where all of you are souls that have come to Earth to accomplish soul growth. If you develop that team consciousness which is lacking on Earth, you will become a great team, the One Human Family team, and it will be *an only team* and *an only family*. It is not about the Turkish family, or the Syrian family or the American family or the African family. It will be only one family of human beings living on planet Earth, and as such you must begin to behave.

Do not forget that work begins with oneself as individual work, and as individual communication with us to enable all of us to work together towards getting Earth out of the chaos in which it is immersed.

Receive my blessings and know that we have pinned all

our hopes on you and on the possibility of finally starting to collaborate – on working together, you and us.

Thank you.

Omstara
(from the constellation Cygnus)

> *Omstara is skilled at examples and exercises. This is one of her best. Play along, take her invitation seriously and you, too, will feel the deep, unshakable bond she speaks of.*
>
> *The experience complements Lady Nada's article on "Compassion Unites the Human Family," although the articles were written four years apart.*

Experience the Hidden Bond

WeSeekToServe Newsletter, June 2018

Omstara

There are many ways of breaking down barriers between peoples. How many things do you and your neighbors have in common with each other ... as well as with those who are not your immediate neighbors?

Parenting? Concern for children even if they are not your own? How many times have strangers smiled and inquired about an infant in arms? "How old?" "What's her name?" "He's a beautiful baby."

I would ask you to imagine with me for a moment. Imagine other situations, situations of concern. Concern for those who are trapped in earthquake rubble. Concern for those unable to escape a flash flood.

How often do those who are trapped ask their rescuers for credentials? Do they ask what religion their rescuers practice, what organizations they do or do not belong to? Do you imagine anyone asking what political party their rescuer voted for before they accepted the offered help?

If you were the rescuer, what credentials would you collect before you agreed to the rescue?

The reason there are times when you do not ask for credentials is that there exists an inherent bond among members of the human family of Earth. And with all the divisive issues that have arisen, it takes an infant, a child or an emergency to activate that unquestioning bond. This is nothing new. There are bonds of life. Consider those who would rescue animals in this flood I have conjured. There is a bond with living creatures, particularly if they are infant creatures.

I would invite you to imagine with me, invite you to recognize the bond I speak of for what it is when you feel it. I would ask you to take each situation I have named. Relax, imagine and let yourself experience the bond you feel.

- *You are on a shady bench, holding the infant. You are the stranger pausing to admire the child.*

- *You are trapped in earthquake rubble – alone in the dark. You are the rescuer heaving debris aside because you hope someone is there, still alive.*

- *You and your child or your grandchild or your grandmother are on the roof praying for help as floodwaters rage. You are in a boat dressed for the weather, out to help people who are stranded.*

Think of yourself in other situations, joyous or frightening. Think of yourself on each side of each situation. Let yourself imagine, let yourself feel. And then examine your feelings. Let them flow through you and you will begin to understand the ties that bind the human family together ... because you have let yourself recognize and experience those ties.

Extend again. I ask you now to consider this bond extending to those of us from off Earth. We have young ones. We face emergencies. We have come to Earth in an effort to help.

Why this exercise? We who are your off-world cousins, we who are the elders of the human family of Earth – we are asking that you send unconditional love into the network that binds the entire human family of Earth together, and binds the family of Earth to the human families of those from off Earth.

Once you feel that bond, help strengthen it. Send love into the energetic network that creates that bond you have experienced. You will not find this network in your science books. But if you have played along with me, you know that bond is there.

With unconditional love,

Omstara
(from the constellation Cygnus)

> *Omstara speaks of preparing for the day when the question of life on other planets is no longer a question.*

Open Heart and Mind to What Will Be
WeSeekToServe Newsletter, July 2018

Omstara

As the *Ageless Wisdom Evolving* series unfolds and as we, your Off-Earth Allies, speak on this forum, you will be learning more and more about life as it exists for those of us off Earth. You will learn from our observations of off-Earth beings that you have not yet met and you will find that there are commonalities that are shared even with life forms that are on the surface quite different from those of Earth.

But that is by way of what will be coming eventually. For now, let us focus on your life today. Having heard a bit about the common human culture that spans the universe and about redefining the concept of life itself,[2] you may well be wondering where you belong and what you can do to make the future more secure ... for yourself, for the loved ones you are responsible for and indeed, for the planet itself.

For one thing, you can absorb the fact that much of your society, its structures and conditionings are irretrievably broken. A very small and privileged minority is holding on for dear life, but for the rest, it is time to move on – onward and upward. It is like a snake at molting time, when the skin no longer fits, however useful and comfortable it has been. It is time to embrace the winds of change and discard all that is obsolete, useless and ultimately unhealthy to cling to in your crumbling civilization. Make up your mind to embrace change and not cower in fear as to what may lay beyond.

For another, you can begin to trust yourself and your

---

[2] In this newsletter, Master Teachers Venetian from Earth and Ondru from Sirius speak to the topics Omstara refers to. It is altogether a mind-expanding newsletter!

Email ReadingsFromSharonK@gmail.com if you would like a copy of the July, 2018 WSTS newsletter.

heart to be sound. Do you think you were put here now or that you elected to come to Earth at this time for no special reason? That it is all an accident or what you refer to as a crap shoot? What did the first gilled fish know as they left the water to learn to walk on land, and yet they did so – armed, prepared and fully capable to adapt did they but heed the call.

You too are part of a great leap forward for planet Earth at this time, or can be ... no less than the taming and reorientation of the heart faculty – your heart faculty and your mind. You are here to open the doors of perception and learn to think in new ways, to align with broader human faculties developing now worldwide. Thousands upon thousands of groups, large and small, under whatever guise or by whatever practices, are undergoing intense, voluntary training in mind expansion, learning to "think with the heart and feel with the mind."

A worldwide awakening is indeed underway. As your educational and centuries-old belief systems crumble, as your scientific discoveries race ahead of themselves, take heed. Can you not hear us, your solar and galactic allies, knocking at the door? We come bearing gifts to help get you through this awkward stage.

Perhaps not so many of you yet have come face to face with members of our many groups of off-Earth Allies here to assist. You may not see us but you can reach out with your minds and open to our friendship. That is how it starts – heart to heart and mind to mind – for in these two dimensions we are already close, much closer than you can imagine. We meet in the halls of intuition, and thousands of groups worldwide are seeking to establish contact in these realms. Join them! Actively develop your intuition by whatever means you choose, preferably in a group setting for that is swiftest.

Be part of the vanguard, bringing to that growing assembly all of the sound mind qualities and goodwill that are yours to muster. Forget despair. Let go the old skin, cracked and damaged and useless that it is. You know better, and you know you know better, and that you have a role to play in a great leap forward for humanity. It is no accident that you are here and that we too, from the greater universe, await you on this threshold. Soon we will no longer be hidden in plain sight, soon we will be celebrating together your re-integration into your cosmic home and family.

Open your hearts, open your minds. Take with us those first steps into the new world that awaits you. Alongside your elders from the Community, we watch. We await your widespread welcome. We shall not lead you astray.

Your friend and ally, speaking for the many,

Omstara
(from the constellation Cygnus)

> *Omstara, as an Off-Earth Ally who is here to assist the human family in a rapid consciousness expansion, speaks of the gift we have of self-placed limits and free will.*

What Limits Have You Set?
WeSeekToServe Newsletter, August 2018

Omstara

Dear Friends,

I greet you with all my heart and address you today as an observer from a constellation afar, yes, but one who is deeply committed to your progress and wellbeing on all fronts. The crux of the matter concerning life and evolutionary progress on planet Earth is that you, as members of the human family of Earth, are endowed with life and have the gift of free will to govern it with. Each of you, as a living, breathing human being, is a cosmic experiment in free will.

Can you understand and accept this premise, that you are a cosmic experiment on this planet at this time? How buried are you in family dysfunction or traditions, the constraints of your occupation or the shortcomings in your life circumstances and opportunities? How much of your life did you simply fall into as convenient? Or perhaps you have been swept into some aspect of the trauma and tragedy running rampant at this time. There have been dark days all throughout history, so trouble is nothing new. Still, how much are you wrapped up in your mindset and day-to-day or long-term problems, unable to comprehend how precious life is, how precious *your* life is?

What limits have you placed on yourself, and more importantly, what mark do you want to make in life? I am not talking glibly of wealth or fame or celebrity, which bear their own lessons, but in terms of actual advancement in the quality of life on your Earth. Please think about that. Think about how you can be the best example of a human being and give shape to your highest values and aspirations.

In other words, live your life as your soul would have you

live it, for in so doing, you have a chance to contribute not only to yourself, your family, your society and the human race in general, but to the greater universe itself. Lofty words perhaps, I know, but I urge you to direct and fill your life to the fullest and best. It is your gift and your sacred duty.

So what then is this glorious and very specific boon called free will that is yours, hopefully to make the best you can of this life for yourself and others? Do you understand what power it confers? Many do not, and many cannot. Many are brutally engaged with just surviving day to day while many others, provided with adequate and even bountiful food, sanitation, etc. take these advantages for granted but cling to some other, often self-imposed limitation and languish in spiritual bankruptcy.

The fact is that both the haves and have-nots on this planet share the particular gift of life, and many of the "haves" are have-nots – just as starving in terms of directing, inhabiting and fulfilling their lives as are those others who have not food, or shelter or other basic wherewithal to physically survive.

This world in many ways is spiritually starving whereas the banquet of life is there in all its splendor. What is it that will nourish your soul? That will bring you to the understanding of what a great and precious gift it is to be alive and in position to help fulfill the divine plan for this, your Mother Earth?

Treat wisely these gifts, my friends. Please seek out ways in which you can use your life and your free will to help balance out the negative energies on this world for your life and contribution matter. Truly, they do.

Your loving friend and partner,

Omstara
(from the constellation Cygnus)

> *Omstara, with one of her exercises, leads us to examine the pillars of belief that we rely on. Some of these pillars, she suggests, might need dusting to remind us they exist, refurbishment perhaps or even repair.*

Pillars of Belief
WeSeekToServe Newsletter, October 2019

Omstara

Dear Readers,

The pillars that get you through a day feeling comfortable moving forward or stepping aside, whatever your decisions are for the day – these pillars that you don't think about often are the pillars that enable you to make these decisions with ease, comfort and confidence. I would say these are the pillars of your belief system. The question is: Have you dusted them lately? Have you looked at them lately? Is it necessary to review them? Are there any cracks that need examination?

It is an analogy but I think you understand where I am going. In this time on this planet, there is a great deal of chaos. There is certainty on one hand and there is uncertainty on the other. There is polarization.

Belief systems, your personal belief system, may or may not be stretched, may or may not need a few modifications to help you navigate the whitewater that seems to be coming closer and closer to many people. I would advise you in this time, if you can possibly arrange it, to sit down and list three beliefs that you consider to be unchangeable, without need to question, beliefs that will stand by you, that you can rely on no matter what is coming down the road. Three.

I would ask you to list three more but I would have these last three be beliefs that you feel might indeed be subject to change. If not change, upgrade – more clarification, modification in some way. This need not be tossing them out. It might be strengthening them, refining them, broadening them. But these are three perhaps for total refurbishment.

When you sit down to do this, the first three I would have you take a look at to see how long you have held this belief, where it came from, what it adheres to in this day and age, how it applies. What part of this day and age does it support and apply to?

And for the next three, you could ask the same questions. How long have you held this belief? Where did it come from? You have already decided by putting it in this category that it needs some kind of modification given today's environment. And when I say "today's environment," I mean your total personal environment ... which starts with you in the center. Where you live, work, eat; your closest family and friends, your work colleagues. It starts there and goes all the way to the entire population of the world.

The purpose of this exercise is to remind you to take the time you need for yourself and your own centered stability as the world may shift and heave around you. That is the purpose of this exercise.

I would also have you enjoy, a peaceful, heart-reflective enjoyment, the pleasure of taking this look at who you are and how you are navigating this incarnation.

That is what I have to say.

I thank you very much.

Omstara
(from the constellation Cygnus)

> *Omstara once again presents a thought-provoking exercise. This time she suggests two lists at year end – neither one of them the traditional resolutions.*

Not Your Traditional New Year's Resolutions

WeSeekToServe Newsletter, December 2019

Omstara

Dear Readers,

The year-end celebrations are upon us. This is the time for joy and for retrospection, so I would give you some advice with a heartfelt smile and encouragement.

As you celebrate the close of this year, I would ask you not for a list of the traditional resolutions – what you're going to do more of or less of in the coming year – no, that is not what I would ask you to consider.

You who are lightworkers, you who are growing spiritually, you whose minds are open to the expansion of your awareness, the expansion of your consciousness both in the dense physical and in the spiritual ... I would smile with you and be with you at your shoulder as you celebrate the conclusion of this year.

The list I would ask you to make is a list of those events, those relationships, the progress – whatever it might be that you plan to celebrate with joy at the end of the coming year ... make a list for yourself of those things, and keep that list in your heart for the entire year. "These are the things I wish to celebrate at the end of the coming year." And let that list guide your decisions, your actions in the coming year. Make it a thoughtful list, a list that inspires your heart, a list that you look forward to celebrating with satisfaction.

And I would ask you, within this list some place, to make room for something unanticipated. And to make an entry for what you will celebrate that happened for someone near and dear to you, be it a child, a spouse, a parent, a cousin, a very dear friend, a colleague ... someone you would like to see celebrating next year-end with joy.

If this is your guide, your mindset for the coming year, you will have an open mind to progress, to growth, to the unanticipated and how that can enrich your experience in the year to come.

That is my wish for you.

Your friend,

Omstara
(from the constellation Cygnus)

LADY NADA

Lady Nada's focus is the healing of deep spiritual wounds, spiritual misdirection and schisms outside humanity's mainstream religions.

My Icon
It is known that I work and serve as a healer. But what kind of healer? Well, I bring light to the dark. I bring knowledge to the ignorant, knowledge that serves to heal the rifts. And I have been doing this with humanity for a very long span of time. Therefore, my icon of an ancient lantern in the dark perfectly expresses my line of work. Not only do I bring that to you, but I also show that to you.

Lady Nada was one of the first nine teachers to begin Panel Discussions on WeSeekToServe.com. It is clear that she cares deeply about incarnate humanity, especially those who have experienced and freed themselves from uncomfortable group persuasion. The healer that she is comes through to me in her channeling frequency. I find that I respond comfortably to the metaphors and images she uses as she teaches.

Lady Nada Bio

Current Focus
As I said, I am a healer. Specifically I attend the threads that bind humanity together, for there is a direct line to the heart and mind. Therefore I am working with thoughts and with information ... thus also with *lack* of thought and with *mis*information. Many ancient rifts are based on wrong thought and misinformation. It takes skillful and patient guidance to help the truth gain light in this kind of dark, to gain light in the heart of one who feels they have been wronged and someone must pay a debt.

The human family of Earth would be in an ongoing "spin-cycle" of tit-for-tat – ongoing and unstoppable – if left without guidance towards the light of truth. So much beauty and connection is lost when getting even is all one can see or focus on.

So, I shine a light in that place of dark thought, that place of misguided intent, in hope of an eventual outcome of reconciliation and healing. Once the light has been recognized, my task becomes easier, for those who accept this moment of recognition can usually take it from there on the path of healing. Alas, the heavy burden to get them up the hill to see the light is where I practice my healing craft.

That kind of healing is my focus, in addition to what is more normally under the umbrella of healing.

Favorite or Significant Past Life
In keeping with the current times, I would take this opportunity to express the importance of balance. Lives where I learned the most, lives that I hold the most precious are not necessarily lives of recognition or fame, but lives where I could balance my feminine experiences by incarnating as masculine.

There is much to learn in being a full-fledged human, much to learn about Earth's two main avenues of expression. I was fortunate to have very insightful learning, healing lives as a woman contrasted with very active-oriented lives as a man.

When I look back, I realize how different these lives were and how much I appreciated the lessons learned from each. In short, I loved being a man and I loved being a woman. Perhaps because I currently have a feminine filter, I can say that I appreciate my masculine lives as I miss what they brought to the table.

Humans are lucky in that they can experience each of these views along the way and have the opportunity to bring the strengths of each together in an uncountable variety of ways, thus making each human, in sum total, a truly unique expression.

> *In the inaugural issue of MasterSpeak, the name chosen for WeSeekToServe.com Panel Discussions, Lady Nada speaks of expanding consciousness inward to the soul.*
>
> *Note that in the very first issue two Master Teachers use different fine-tuned definitions of "consciousness." The way they work together respecting these differences is what they wished to demonstrate with the Panel Discussions, although I doubt they deliberately created a difference for the inaugural issue.*

Consciousness

WeSeekToServe.com Panel Discussion, January 2012

Lady Nada

I too would speak on consciousness. I would speak on consciousness as a feedback loop between the "separated self" and the rest of existence. That feedback loop functions between – let us call it a self-contained body – between a self-contained body and the *entire rest of existence,* to the far reaches of the cosmos. And that is just the dense physical plane.

I will agree with Master Kuthumi that there is awareness and interaction with the environment. That will do, I have no objection to that definition. You will find, you who read MasterSpeak, that we do not always totally agree. We do, however, respect each other's opinions, and we do respect the fact that there are differences of perspective on any given topic.

What resonates with one may not resonate with another. But we do respect each other. This is one feature it would be well for humanity to duplicate, but I shan't go further.

I am talking about you as a body interacting with everything else – everything and everyone else: consciousness, awareness, sometimes called self-awareness. But there is "self-aware" and "awareness of the not-self" and then we get into philosophical arguments that I am not going to venture into. I am more concerned about the way consciousness (be it awareness, interaction or a combination) can work two ways.

Consciousness Directed Inward

I am sure that you have heard of going inward to your inner self, inward to your true self, inward until you touch the spark of God inside, until you touch your soul. And from there, new levels of awareness emerge. You become conscious that there is even more to life, there is more to interact with than the tables, the chairs, the birds, the trees, the grass, the sky, etc.

You have the ability for inward interaction, and expansion of consciousness inward until you reach the still, small voice of your soul within. When you reach that voice of your soul within, you may find that you have direct contact with a driving force that has led you to where you are today.

You do things, and you say, "Well, I had a feeling," or you may call it instinct or you may call it intuition. No matter what you call it, you have experienced knowing without knowing, knowing without thinking, a knowing without a mental analysis. The subconscious is turned inward and you find a fount of wisdom, of guidance that flows outward and can direct your life.

The difference as your consciousness expands, is that what was at one time just a feeling, by whatever name, can become a turning inward, can become an understanding that within each of you is the spark of God that is your soul. That soul is waiting and hoping and probably sending out messages saying, "Call me. Ask me. I am here!"

When you can develop the feel, the *knowing* of a regular contact with this soul inside, you have reached the point where your consciousness is expanding inward, and through expanding inward, it is broadening and becoming much, much, *much* larger. For your soul has lifetimes of wisdom to draw upon. Your soul has set intentions for this life and what it hoped to accomplish.

Guidance That Does Not Fail

You have free will, you may do as you choose, but the soul had hopes when you were born. The soul had a plan. Through expanding your consciousness – your awareness, your ability to interact – and directing this inward to communication with that soul, you will find a guidance that will not fail you.

You have other guides, you all have other guides. But they work with you by permission and arrangement with your soul, so your soul is the CEO and the COO and the CFO and whatever other chief of something that you can name. So why not go to the head guy, why not go to the head gal?

Find the way through meditation, through silence, through other means that may be yours personally to formulate a direct communication with your soul. And let your consciousness expand to the point where you can have a conversation with your own soul and know where it is that your soul intended this life to go.

That would be my comments on consciousness. The environment is not only outside, the environment is inside, and you can interact with the director and the author of the life plan that was given when you were born.

Thank you,

Lady Nada

> *Lady Nada provides us with an overview of soul evolution that has clear imagery, is easy to understand and is technically accurate. It is a comfortable article for those who are in the early stages of exploring reincarnation. One can learn a great deal more and fit the details into the model Lady Nada has given us here.*
>
> *Mother Mary also spoke on this panel and uses a metaphor we can all understand to explain the concept of soul evolution.*

Soul Evolution

WeSeekToServe.com Panel Discussion, February 2012

Lady Nada

What I have to say on the evolution of the soul is this – think of walking a pattern. Start off in a straight line. Then step to the right, and keep turning right and keep turning right again until you have made a full circle and are back to the line you were walking.

Continue to walk straight.

After walking straight for a while, you will turn left. Keep turning left. Take steps and angle left. Keep turning left and keep turning left until such time as you are back on the line you were walking. Then again walk straight on that line.

Then repeat the pattern – turning right and turning right and turning right until you are back on the line, and walk the straight line. Then turn left and left and left.

Now, imagine that at the end of this walk, there is a destination. You have a start and you have a finish.

This line is soul evolution. Every loop you make is an incarnation.

The straight line is the time in between incarnations. When you turn left, you become one gender, when you turn right, you incarnate as the other gender. If your line is balanced, you have as many loops on the left as you have on the right. Many souls do not do this. Many souls prefer to always turn right – or 80% of the time – and only occasionally venture into the left. Or it could be the other way around.

But that is the continuity, because every time you

venture off that straight line – that between-lives line – to incarnate, by the time you work your way back to the line, you bring with you experiences. Now with some of these experiences you look back and say, "Well that was not so good," and you have something that you would like to balance – a relationship that did not go right, a decision that was not in the best interest of your forward motion.

The length of your "walk" between lives will vary. It may be a long time and it may be a short time. There are various reasons. But this walk between lives is not how the soul evolves. This is an image of an evolving soul, so that you understand the between-lives thread – and it is more than a thread, it is actually a between-lives wide pathway that is complex in its own right.

Every time you venture into incarnation with one of those loops that starts at birth and loops and loops and loops, and ends with the death of the body – this is not the death of the soul. You simply end up where you started, back in the between-lives state.

Now focus on that point where you left the between-lives state, went into incarnation, had all of these experiences, a whole lifetime of experiences, and came back to the between-lives state. So picture yourself looping out and around and returning to the same node where you left the between-lives state.

Let us focus on the node of departure and return. If you focus on that node and put it under your microscope as it were, you will find that before you left the between-lives state there was planning. And when you return from the incarnated state, there is assessment. So there is a lot going on in that node of departure and return.

Now we come to evolution. The incarnated state is a classroom. It is a learning. It is an opportunity to fulfill the plan that you devised before you left the between-lives state. Now part of the soul *remains* in that between-lives state, part of the soul is always within that pathway of return, return to the Divine. The more influence the soul that remains in the between-lives state has on each incarnation, the more completely the plan for that life is fulfilled. And the more completely the plan for that life is fulfilled, the more ambitious the plan can be for the next life. The more advancement there can be between lives.

This has to do with the communication and the interaction between the soul that remains in what I have called the between-lives state and the aspect of that soul in the incarnated state. Now how much of the soul comes down into the incarnated state and how much stays in the between-lives state? That, too, depends on a matter of soul evolution.

When a soul, which is Divine by definition, starts off on this journey, only a very, very thin thread is influential in the incarnated state. So one could say that only a small portion of the Divine soul is noticed. During the next incarnation, and the next, and the next, as more and more communication is established with the incarnated state, then the soul in the between-lives state is more involved in the life of its incarnated self.

As you near your destination, there is such fullness of communication that the soul can divide itself equally between what is in the between-lives state and what comes down to the incarnated state. Water leveling, as it were, so that the incarnation is simply an eddy and the surface remains the same. The degree of soul influence remains the same in both the incarnated state and the between-lives state.

The closer you come to the Divine, the less you are able to distinguish, the less the soul is able to distinguish between itself in the between-lives state and itself in its incarnated state. Because now, in the incarnated state, the soul is living what it truly is – a Divine spark of God.

Those who are incarnated can spot those people and know that they are giving off the Light of God in their very lives. That is the picture I would paint of soul evolution.

I hope that this is helpful.

My blessings on you all,

Lady Nada.

> *Every soul is born with portions of both divine masculine and divine feminine energy. Yet it is only when women gain cultural equality of respect, when women and men each stand comfortably in their personal power respecting the contributions of one another that the divine aspects of masculine and feminine energies can balance and manifest to serve the human family.*
>
> *Lady Nada speaks of the consequences gender balance and imbalance have on soul growth and the divine aspects of masculine and feminine energies.*

The Vital Role of Gender Equality

WeSeekToServe Newsletter, September 2018

Lady Nada

In the coming months, we encourage you to pay attention to headlines in the world's news for they will include many stories involving women and their struggles for fairness and justice. As the "weaker" sex, women have been prey to many ills throughout history, yet it has not been this way in every culture.

We would like to highlight cultures where men and women have enjoyed a much closer bond of autonomy and interaction, independence and cooperation. For in these cultures, it is understood that what women bring to the culture is different but equally as important as the contribution of men. What women bring to the table is the very foundation of every culture. And indeed, the fact remains that women give birth to culture through their tireless actions of nurturing their children and families.

It is strange to conceive that this needs to be highlighted and explained, for it is an obvious and indelible fact. Lacking however are the respect and recognition of women that are reserved for some deities whereas these considerations should in fact be extended to every woman.

The soul has lessons to be learned throughout its long sojourn, including learning how to wield with integrity both masculine energy and feminine energy alike. Each energy brings a different quality to complete the whole, yet depending on what culture one is born into, that lesson can be a contradiction, a very rough example of these qualities. Remember, integrity is a distinctive quality one needs to master in the form of both masculine and feminine energy.

The pathway to achieving this goal is to understand the working puzzle, the plan for humanity, and that its ultimate purpose and modus operandi are to experience both sides of the coin, all angles of perception – young/old, male/female, religious/atheistic, etc. True experience, or walking in one's own shoes is the only correct and cohesive pathway to learn and gain valuable perspective concerning inbred influences, prejudices and biases.

Ultimately, having compassion to each and every other person's pathway and part of the whole can lead you to understand your own place in the story.

In times past, when survival was more precarious, every member of a community was considered with appropriate honor and regard, for each depended upon and contributed to the survival of the group. Women's tasks were different from men's, as they are now, but not de-valued. Rather, they were considered an essential part of the chain of activity. Women have always had the intrinsic task of birthing and nurturing the coming generation, and there can be no more sacred a task. It is a service to humanity that plays out in many forms of activity, not just the birth process. It is also the wielding of feminine energy.

Having said this, the divine masculine is equally important though for different reasons, creating the very need for reincarnating souls to experience both the divine masculine and the divine feminine. Each is a part of the whole, not an enemy to disregard or devalue for their needs or abilities.

The imbalance in one's regard towards the opposite sex as portrayed in some cultures today is vastly different from the norm that was present in some cultures of humanity's past – cultures where men and women toiled with esteem for each other's skills and abilities, where women's birthright was to be considered rulers and equals, where both sexes were honored and valued for their special gifts and contributions.

The fight for this balance has taken a deeper turn of late and traction is changing the tides. But the fight is not over yet nor will it be so easily won, for many have been very comfortable in their position of power over others.

Let it be known that much divine energy is behind this movement to equalize the feminine in the eyes of the masculine. Let it also be known that many have already realized this and therefore set the example, but old thoughts remain and are difficult to change and expand. Know too that the light is spreading.

Lady Nada

> *Lady Nada wished to speak on the panel that responded to the reader who puzzled about the existence of so many gods. Her explanation, seemingly obvious on the surface, holds true even as one gathers more and more details about the workings of the cosmos.*
> *Quan Yin and Mother Mary also spoke on this panel.*

Many Traditions – Many Gods
WeSeekToServe.com Panel Discussion, May 2012

Lady Nada

Now the work I do is healing, and it is healing of various religious injuries. We shall simply call them mental-emotional injuries, hindrances to individual spiritual maturity. I work on healing those scars, from this life or past lives, that the soul may move forward on its journey to reunification with the Divine.

What does this have to do with all the gods in all the various religions? Well, it has to do with healing effects of any of these gods who endorses violence and vengeance against other human beings or other gods, for vengeance is not part of the Divine Plan. So it is healing those effects. What does that healing entail? I will not go into that here. I will leave that to the reader's imagination. The point is, vengeance and violence are not part of the Divine.

Now take your daily life. You have many roles in your daily life. Chances are, you have a great many roles.

You interact one way as a child, one way as part of a distant family network, one way as a spouse, one way as a parent, one way as an employee, one way as an employer, one way as a friend, one way as a new acquaintance. All these different ways of interacting and relationships I shall call aspects of who you are.

You bring out one aspect of who you are if you are working with a coworker. This need not be paid employment, simply that you and someone else are working together to accomplish something. It may be spring cleaning. It may be cleaning up after a flood. It does not matter. You are working together for some purpose. You have a relationship and you behave in a certain manner for this relationship.

You have another relationship with a very dear and close friend, a friend you can take your troubles to, a friend who brings their troubles to you. This is another aspect of your relationship, and it is quite different from the relationship you have if you are trying to accomplish something specific with a coworker.

If you are ill, you have a relationship with your doctor or your healer. For a day or two, think about all the different aspects of who you are that you take out into the world.

Now, it is the same with our one Creator, our one Source, our one God. There are many, many different aspects and qualities, because there are many aspects to Creation, and yet it is all One, just as you are one even if you have different aspects for different situations.

That is how Oneness works. That is how the Creator works. Many, many different aspects, but all One. Always One. And the more intimate you become with your soul and the spark of God within, the more intimate you become with the Divine, so that you recognize the Divine in all its different aspects. I would have you consider that as you consider the many, many different gods that are created, worshipped, and spoken of, in all the religious schools of thought that have been, are, and will be.

Spiritual healing takes place when you do as my colleagues have recommended and look inward to your own Divine self, and ask yourself, "What functions, what qualities do I see in this god or this god or this god, that are healthy for the whole of Oneness?"

If the qualities are healthy for the whole of Oneness, chances are they are an aspect of the one God, and that means those aspects are within you. You can ask yourself, "Which of these aspects can I manifest and contribute to the health and well-being of the whole? Of the One? Of the part of Creation that I inhabit at the moment?"

I would ask you, again, to take a day or two or three and think of how many aspects of your "oneself" that you express as you go through your daily life, and relate that to the various aspects the one Source that have been deified. Ask which of these aspects – your own or those of the various deities named, listed and understood to be deities – which aspects contribute to the healing of the whole, contribute to a healthy environment of the whole, where everyone has an opportunity to experience their own spiritual growth?

Each one of you reading this contributes to the environment in which all others are able to experience spiritual maturing.

What is your contribution? And are you satisfied with it?

Thank You,

Lady Nada

> *Lady Nada once again uses an easy-to-understand metaphor to shed light on the street fighting that seeks to win and command people's hearts, minds and obedience. Her focus is healing souls injured in the fight.*
>
> *This article and Mother Mary's article on "Spiritual Enfranchisement" complement one another.*

Street Fighting and the New Civilization
WeSeekToServe.com Panel Discussion, January 2013

Lady Nada

We are speaking this month of street fighting. I would venture that everyone who is reading this has their own idea of what street fighting is, and where it takes place – in movies, for example, or possibly in another part of town.

Street fighting is not an innocuous term that is limited to this place or that place, or to this neighborhood or that neighborhood. It is a pervasive human condition, which I believe my colleagues have demonstrated in all that they have said.

I would return to the healing that calls me most, the healing that calls me into action in the human realm. That healing, the healing that speaks to my heart, when traced to its ultimate source, leads to a school of thought, a philosophy, a religion, a belief system, a certainty – an absolute certainty – that *these* words, *this* dogma, *this* liturgy, *this* outlook, is The One Way to live, The One Way to survive on the physical plane, The One Way to have an afterlife, to be assured of grace from the Divine.

There is always a reward laid out. If this-that-or-the-other is done, and done properly, as designed by those who have long since ceased to breathe, then this-or-that is the result. The result is always a reward. If this-or-that is not done, then there is punishment, specific or implied.

Part of choosing to live your life according to these rules – this dogma, this doctrine – this righteousness that you know in your heart is the correct recipe, is the expectation that you will receive your reward. And if yours is the correct recipe – very likely granted by God, the Divine – and if the reward for a life lived in accordance with this recipe is true, then part of your responsibility is to bring all those with whom you have contact into alignment with this way of thinking. You do that because you love them, because you want them to find in their lives the certainty and the peace and calm in the center that you have found in your own life.

There is no room in these rigid approaches, these formulaic approaches, there is no room to include those who do not fit into that formula, those for whom that formula is not comfortable.

If you look at everything from radio waves to microwaves, you understand that there are different frequencies. And frequencies explain a great deal.

Why is blue your favorite color rather than green or red or orange or yellow? Each color has a frequency, a vibration, and people respond to these colors in different ways. Each school of thought, each philosophy has its own vibration, its own frequency, and people respond in different ways, just as they respond differently to colors. Colors shall be my metaphor.

Now, if you like and respond to bright orange and do not want red in your life, and if one of your friends responds most favorably to blue and does not care for yellow, does that make one of you right and the other one wrong? I think most of you will agree that it does not. There is something inherent in each response – something perhaps soul-deep, for souls, too, respond to frequencies – and if the response is not inherent, there is some reason for it.

Yet if someone responds to blue and is told that yellow is the *only* right color, is the only right frequency, then they are not comfortable. And if they are told: "Comfortable or not, you must live in yellow. You must be yellow. You must think yellow. You must wear yellow. You must *preach* yellow," when all the while their heart longs for blue, they can be damaged, because there is nothing wrong with blue.

I use this as an example because, you see, forcing yellow on someone who responds to blue is one of humanity's most insidious street fights. It is the group, the body of knowledge, the historic precedent, the putative word of God embodied in yellow being forced and force-fed to one whose experience of God is through the color blue.

It is the forced decision to be "yellow" that distorts the living, incarnational experience of the soul. It is the rigid insistence on "yellow" that distorts and injures the incarnated being. This can go on incarnation after incarnation, and it is those distortions, that street fighting – the powerful group against the individual – that forces the individual into submission, or perhaps drives them away, psychologically injured, to fare as best they can as a maimed and injured being, knowing in their heart that whatever there was in that group was not right for them. They look in the mirror and see only someone who does not belong.

These are the kinds of street fights that I work to heal, the street fights of individuals – or, if they are fortunate, a small group of individuals – who have been injured by a larger group. Whether they stay or whether they leave this powerful group, they have been injured in a street fight.

It could be that the soul within them called out to be free and they were not able to break free. That is a street fight between one Spark of God from within contending with a dictatorial group.

I think that you can each fill in the blanks and come up with suitable examples. This is an insidious kind of street fighting. It is a street fight that is a power struggle, and the group does not seek power over land, or even power over the individual's possessions. The power these groups win is influence over the decision making capacity of every individual who joins and capitulates even when the group does not speak to their heart. This is an insidious street fight.

What is the remedy?

If the individual is strong enough and sufficiently in touch with their soul and breaks away, that is one thing. But I work with healing the many who were not able, when it would have been time to break away, were not able to do so for whatever reason – for love of a family, for respect due that family, because of a misplaced respect for elders who were trusted. There are many scenarios, many.

But it is still a street fight. It is a street fight for the minds, for the hearts and minds at the deepest level, the spiritual level where one meets the divine Spark of God within.

The remedy for this fight is, as has been shown by my colleagues, a respect, a learning, an acknowledgement that no matter how large the differences, there are commonalities within the One. It can be phrased that there are many paths and many ways, just as there many colors. Red may be a wonderful color for you or it may be a disastrous color for you, one you do not like.

The remedy is acknowledging – every single person acknowledging that the color they personally find difficult to imagine, that color is right for the one who uses it and responds to it. The remedy is to listen and learn, and appreciate that there are differences, pronounced differences. Yet at the core, know in your heart there is only One and there are commonalities to be found.

The remedy is love and patience and respect. The remedy is being true to the Spark of God within you while being fully respectful of the Spark of God within every other individual, knowing that their Spark of God resonates to a different color.

Doesn't that present a beautiful picture of the Divine, that there is room for every nuance of every color in the entire rainbow? And they are all God. They are all One. They are all Divine.

And when all are healed of the trauma of being injured in some way by those who resonate to a different color, then we can live in a complementary environment where the beauty of each color shines in its own place, at its own time, in its own way. And every individual can admire the beauty in all colors, including the ones they do not resonate with.

The street fighting for spiritual, philosophical supremacy will end. Humanity will find the total joy and appreciation of the variety that will emerge as we realize there are many, many colors, each with its own nuance, each with its own beauty.

And please know, always, that none of the beauty elsewhere diminishes the beauty that you hold within you.

This knowledge will be part of the new civilization. Street

fighting for dominance will simply fade away. That is my prediction. That is my healing journey.

I come to heal. I come to focus on those who have been thus injured, that they may find peace and comfort and security in their own unique approach and their own unique manifestation of the God Spark that lives within.

Thank you.

Lady Nada

> *Lady Nada speaks to the contributions we make when we demonstrate compassion with our thoughts alone.*
>
> *This article complements Omstara's exercises enabling us to "Experience the Hidden Bond."*

Compassion Unites the Human Family

WeSeekToServe.com Open Forum, September 2014

Lady Nada

Dear Reader,

The Open Forum is an avenue for panelists to present stand-alone subjects dear to us individually. Today, I feel it is my responsibility to talk about the very important emotion called "compassion" ... and the lack of same.

Compassion is not only an emotion, but also one of the most important "glues" cementing the human family. Compassion unites strangers, it makes people act from the heart, with passion, forgetting differences that might divide them if they stopped to think.

Compassionate people walk around on this planet putting themselves in the position of others, lending a hand to those in need.

Compassion gets extended towards nature – makes you want to water a thirsty plant. And of course towards animals, when you rescue a stray puppy or help a tortoise to cross a busy street.

Compassion is the opposite of selfishness. It is the beginning of caring for each and every thing, and the unconscious realization that all is interconnected.

In the July, 2014 Panel Discussion, Sho[3] spoke of energies and how they operate when aligned with the cosmic heart frequency Source intended for humanity. In a way, this Open Forum is an extension of that conversation. There is so

---

[3] Sho, from the Pleiades, is an expert on energies, whether healing, spreading light or clearing dark energies.

much that needs to be considered about one's own actions. No single heartfelt emotion goes unnoticed or remains without effect on the surroundings. So I can't state strongly enough that being compassionate with everybody and all things in dire straits is a first step in assisting unruly, turbulent energies to calm down and transform into grounded and positive energy that can start to heal.

What we see with growing concern in the incarnate human family is a *lack* of compassion when disaster strikes, for example, or when the news reports horrific war crimes and people in front of their TVs shrug their shoulders and say with discouragement, "What can I do?"

We do admittedly observe a growing wave of compassion, part of which is happening with the help of social media. One example is the outcry of people joining the "Bring our girls back home" campaign to save the kidnapped girls in Nigeria.

This is something we want to bring across to you all. Compassion. Be compassionate, send out love and healing to everything and everybody in need that you come across or hear of. Compassion will eventually lead to passionate action, shaking up those who have gotten out of sync with the cosmic heartbeat.

It is our goal to wake up and shake up each and every one who is bringing suffering and heartache into this world. It is our hope to turn these people around, to make them see how wrong they are, how much they are hurting themselves, and see the wealth of loving and caring alternatives there are for a peaceful community life. Yes, people must learn to see themselves as One and see that there are alternatives and then, after they see, to tread a different path.

Please keep in mind the energetic consequences of every little thought you have about a given situation. When watching the news, do not look away, do not fall into depression but send compassionate, loving energy to everyone involved to help them re-align with the cosmic heart frequency. This may sometimes prove harder than you think, but as with everything, practice makes perfect.

On behalf of your many friends and allies, I thank you for your interest and participation. It is very precious to know that readers of this website are walking the path of raising the planet's consciousness and vibration side by side with us.

Thank you for your compassion. I feel how much each and every one of you cares.

With much love,

Lady Nada

> *Lady Nada addresses the love of souls who stay together one lifetime after another. Mother Mary also spoke on this panel. She explores the interdependence of self-love, love of the other and love of the whole.*

Together We Love

WeSeekToServe.com Panel Discussion, November 2013

Lady Nada

Truly, we can begin here with some thoughts towards our gaining ground in all avenues regarding the process of love, respect and inter-relations between different parties. The test of time is met with this standard, is it not?

There has been much spoken about simple love between any two parties, but I wish to focus on the in-depth spiritual love that spans lifetimes and in fact engages souls to joint action again and again. For this direct, spiritual love between parties binds, ties parties together in union and circumstance. It is not just some breeze passing in the wind.

Soul love is a challenging action that puts the participants to a higher test than circumstantial love. This love has its own direction and plan rather than a random walk down a path for a while. It is the enduring, searing connection that links souls on their joint journeys, compelling them in a focused manner to make their mark.

Whether male or female, adult or child, father, mother, daughter, son or cousin, this cohesive relationship of soul-bonding love interplays in your culture as a lesson pad for those who are engaged in it. The binding love pulls the karmic situations to the fore, inspiring the parties to deal with the energies, for love is an attracting force. It draws one to the other with an almost uncontrollable pull. This magnetic attraction is a manifested law of nature.

While the parties involved experience a range of emotional yearnings, flutterings, pains and joys, these workings are purely a law of nature meant to elicit the bond of love. This bond is mutable but not breakable in the way things are broken. A transmutation may in one lifetime be bridged by certain circumstances, but this bridge will lead to a new resting ground to stand upon in another lifetime.

This type of love has a purpose, a plan, a mission of sorts. It blends the parties forever in awareness of the other, like a signal being activated when the other is near. The magnetic pull is so strong as to activate long-held memories and recognition factors.

As time speeds up, those connected by love will feel increasingly drawn to one another to work through karmic details and clear up their karma, thus approaching the changing time with a fresher perspective. We guide those we can to rendezvous with those with whom they have this relationship bond.

The melding of the parties into a unit is a natural progression. Characteristics intermingle and a true blending occurs that ranges from subtle adaption to character absorption. The range is infinite.

Love is an energy and its pull is a guiding force to those involved. We watch and guide with the intention of helping these parties meet each other lifetime after lifetime, drawn in by the Law of Attraction.

The binding force of such love is unmistakable. We recognize it around us and it has the offshoot reaction to brighten our moods and attitudes. The energetic exchange releases energy that can be detected by others by its infectious effect.

We work hard to guide souls to each other to allow this phenomenon to occur. It is building, binding, calming and strengthening. It is the balancing of the pairs of opposites and so much more. Compassion is gained as a result and this lends itself to others. In all its many forms and versions, love is the binding force of the universe that holds us together and carries us through each life.

Lady Nada

> *Lady Nada reports on progress for the Global Network of Light that the teachers introduced in the WeSeekToServe.com Panel Discussion for the September 2016 issue.*
> *Mother Mary also spoke on this panel.*

Planting the Seeds of the New Earth

WeSeekToServe.com Panel Discussion, Spring 2017

Lady Nada

It pleases us immensely to be speaking to you at this time and to be telling you that our words for you are news of a positive nature and reality. We have measured and observed remarkable seeds of change sprouting through the planes that involve humanity and humanity's progress. We feel the need for those who work diligently to put efforts to palm to realize the effect of their actions.

The light is showing, it is gleaming out from corners and bearing its weight in ways that feed the Global Network of Light. The connection is deepening and serving to maintain grip on all who participate in this new practice of giving.

So we thank you all for your efforts and wish to give you this report that the light work has paid off, the light work is sprouting new life and the light work is growing this new life into a stronger unity that will springboard a plethora of fresh new connections ... thus broad-banding the initial connections into something more complete and more strongly connected.

This is the very leverage we need to thrust humanity forward. It is indeed a nurturing factor and by all laws of nature compounds its effects to draw forth permission for our help. In turn, we can compound our efforts to make your work bear deeper yields. And yes indeed, this is worth celebrating and sharing.

My aim is to make clear to you that while much has been accomplished to date and is in practice making inroads towards a brighter future, we need to continue all together in this vein and to further strengthen the light. The sprouts of light need further nurturing to grow and to continue to grow. The growth must go on and reinforce the burgeoning light work.

We pledge our actions to the cause of a better humanity, and this Network of Light is producing the much needed results to truly give hope for humanity's future. The stretch of time from now until this brighter future depends on how much more light we can successfully transmute to alleviate the darkness.

We trust that efforts will remain strong and thus results will follow suit and the world will take on a new and beautiful shape. Please have faith in your power to create the needed light and lead humanity to brighter days.

Thank you,

Lady Nada

> *Lady Nada reveals the joy of living in awareness on her side of the veil and points to the paths and actions that can help us achieve the same joy in our lives. Quan Yin also spoke on this panel.*

The Joy of Living in Awareness
WeSeekToServe.com Panel Discussion, June 2015

Lady Nada

We can only agree with this construct that there is great joy in living in awareness of your soul and purpose, and we wish that all could experience and know this joy partially or in its entirety, which is to say in full consciousness at last.

The common notion of human existence leaves this concept fully available to each and every individual, and yet for the most part, joy remains out of grasp due to ignorance of what, in our realm and from our perspective, is "naturally human."

It is the natural state for the human soul to seek unity, to seek return to Source, to reach out in joy to one another and recognize the connective network that binds all human souls to a common beginning and to a common objective: return to Source.

This commonality unfolds as the common experience of a journey, always with those ahead who are further down the path, those behind who look to you for assistance and those who travel with you at the same pace. That which is in common is ever so much stronger and binding than that which separates. This is the natural human reality, the spiritual reality to be manifested in the dense as the frequency of Mother Earth rises and the awareness of the human family expands to accommodate the ever-rising frequencies of its individual family members.

Members of the human family have much more within reach than they are aware of if they would but let go without fear and rise with the joy of uplifting frequencies. Understanding that concept would change the world on a daily basis.

We on our side of the veil experience this very joy of awareness. For us, joyful awareness creates, builds and provides the structure for life in our realm to persist harmoniously and pursue its various objectives. We nurture this awareness and it in turn nurtures us all along the path of evolution. Matters remain on track and bring about expansion of plan achievement. From within the environment of this healthy and robust joy, we provide our guidance. We move ahead with joy in our hearts and minds, with the very wish to lend our experience to those in our care.

This life of joyful awareness can be yours – if not in fact now, in objectives and in setting foot on the path to achieve those objectives. It is only through this level of joyous existence that life can bear the fruits for which it is intended. I wish for every member of the entire human family to experience this manner of living in the days ahead. We will do all we can as guides to help the family of Earth to reach this goal.

Without joyful awareness, your hearts and minds suffer to unbearable ends and leave no trace of consciousness expansion upon your days. No means are achieved for passage to the new, no doors are opened. It is the opening of doors that leads humanity on the path to days bathed in joy for which there is no comparison.

We urge you to open your hearts and eyes and minds to this awareness, this concept of joy, a joy that expands day by day to a life where you strive towards awareness and communication with your Higher Self and open heart and mind to the existence of the Higher Selves of others. Open awareness with joy to the human family in all its colors and shapes and sizes and ideals and mysteries. There is much to learn, to share and much to benefit all.

It is with deep tenderness that we view our human brethren, cousins and friends. We have followed this incarnation path in older days and we know and understand all too well the difficulties of your lives.

But we also know and understand the great wealth that comes with awareness of your full and true nature as interconnected, loving souls who travel together as one on the journey of return to Source. Maintain a steady course forward, my friends. Travel in joy.

    Lady Nada

ACCESS TO ADDITIONAL INFORMATION

Additional Information for encouragement, inspiration and growth, and exploring the challenges facing humanity today is available for those who would like to know more.

Most of the messages that the Ascended Master Teachers have channeled through the WeSeekToServe team are as valid today as they were when first published. The articles containing these messages provide information, opinions and thought-provoking insights that are not attainable elsewhere.

The WeSeekToServe team offers three sources for additional information:
- Internet Articles
- Newsletter
- Ageless Wisdom Evolving paperbacks and e-books.
- The WeSeekToServe newsletter

Internet Articles

Readers can access ThoughtsFromAMaster.com articles from Master Teacher Yeshua (Jeshua/Jesus of Nazareth) by category as well as by year of publication. Categories:
- Concepts for Spiritual Growth
- Building a New Civilization
- The Other Side of the Veil
- You and Your Soul
- Issues We Face Today

WeSeekToServe.com/.org articles are not yet organized by category as well as by year of publication. Categorization, however, has begun.

The categories from ThoughtsFromAMaster apply and there is one additional category that focus on becoming acquainted with and communicating with the Ascended Master Teachers and Off-Earth Allies.

Initial Index to WeSeekToServe Categories

If you would like a copy of the initial groupings of WeSeekToServe articles by category, title and publication date or if you would like to be notified if/when that list is published, please email ReadingsFromSharonK@gmail.com.

Newsletters
Single copy:
If you wish a copy of one of the newsletters referenced in this book, please email ReadingsFromSharonK@gmail.com.

Subscription:
If you wish to subscribe to the monthly newsletter:
The English newsletter sign-up can be found on *WeSeekToServe.com*.
The Spanish newsletter sign-up can be found on *WeSeekToServe.org*.

Ageless Wisdom Evolving
All books in the Ageless Wisdom Evolving series are available at Amazon.com in paperback and e-book format. Outside the United States, please check with your local Amazon.

For a quick overview of individual Ageless Wisdom Evolving publications, visit SharonKRichards.com.

Classes and Other Information
Current information about classes can be found on SharonKRichards.com.

Feel free to email ReadingsFromSharonK@gmail.com with comments or questions.

About the Editor

Sharon K. Richards

Master Teacher Yeshua (a.k.a. Jesus of Nazareth) took a pre-birth option on Sharon K. Richards and her willingness to channel in this lifetime. When of free will she agreed to channel for him, he led her through an intensive training course, aided by Master Teachers Mother Mary and Kuthumi.

Sharon shares the ups and downs of her journey as well as information that the teachers asked her to include in her book *Voices for the Ascended Masters – Masters don't view channeling the way we do.*

She has become a voice for the Master Teachers' Internet teachings and a voice to deliver new and realigned material via the *Ageless Wisdom Evolving* series of updates for the 21st century.

Today, Sharon has for the first time "gone public" with classes to share what she has learned working with teachers and various beings from other dimensions on and off Earth as well as going public with her channeling skills.

She is doing readings from the Master Teachers and applying techniques Yeshua taught her to remote view into the pre-birth life-planning conferences of those who have questions about their initial plans for this particular life journey. The remote viewing is followed by channeled Q&A with those present at the planning conference.

Sharon continues her support of the Master Teachers' projects and her training continues as well, preparing her for participation in ever more demanding work in both inner and outer planes.

While all work supporting the plan for this planet is deeply rewarding, being a voice for the Master Teachers in the *Ageless Wisdom Evolving* series is on her list of favorite projects.

Current information can be found on her personal website: SharonKRichards.com.

GLOSSARY

Ageless Wisdom – a.k.a. Ancient Wisdom. A body of knowledge that conveys information about the multi-dimensional structure and functioning of the cosmos, the planet Earth, other planets of our star systems and the human kingdom. These teachings explore the multi-dimensional continuum of evolution, the intended harmony of Oneness and the ever-expanding consciousness of existence.

The educational path that Sharon K. Richards traveled emerged from antiquity in the late 19th century with *The Mahatma Letters* of A.P Sinnett. These letters between Sinnett and Master Teachers Kuthumi (then Koot Hoomi) and Morya are preserved in the British Library.

Sinnett worked with Helena Petrovna Blavatsky who is best known for authoring *The Secret Doctrine* and for her work founding the Theosophical Society.

In the early 20th century, Master Teacher Djwhal Khul worked with Alice A. Bailey on a massive body of work and Master Teacher Morya worked with Helena Roerich on *Agni Yoga*, another many-years, multi-volume undertaking.

Other Master Teachers, e.g. Master Teachers St. Germain and Kuthumi, have also worked with channels to publish their teachings and they have active followings.

Many, many teachers, such as Rudolf Steiner, Torkom Saraydarian and Benjamin Crème, built on the work of Blavatsky, Bailey and Roerich, explaining and expanding on the original material as well as adding their own insights about implementation of the teachings in the physical world. There are many, many channels who bring messages from Ascended Master Teachers and our Off-Earth Allies.

In all these ways, the cosmic teachings known throughout our galaxy and beyond are available on Earth.

Ascended Master Teachers - Ascended Master Teachers – also known as the Masters of Wisdom – are those who have completed lessons in the dense physical of Earth and exist in dimensions of higher frequency.

In the time of Atlantis, the teachers descended to walk among humanity and visit with regularity, guiding, advising and teaching. When Atlantis fell, the teachers withdrew to obscure locations in Earth's etheric fields, but did not leave the planet. All these centuries, they have been attempting to guide and protect humanity from beyond the energy veil that separates them from us.

In the late 19th century, the Ascended Master Teachers began to come forward in order to once again make themselves known to many.

In the teachings of Master Teacher Djwhal Khul given to us through Alice A. Bailey in the first half of the 20th century, the teachers were predicted to return to openly walk among us in the year 2025. At the time this book is published, the teachers do intend to return to walk among us to advise, guide and teach. It is only the date that is in question.

Community of Masters – a.k.a. Community of Spiritual Masters. These are umbrella terms for all evolving Earth beings who have completed lessons and karmic balance on the dense physical plane. Many members within the Community are not actually Master Teachers, including members who have newly completed their physical plane lessons, those who are further down the spiritual path than the Master Teachers, those who have not yet been asked to assume the responsibilities of a Master Teacher and a goodly number of Off-Earth Allies.

etheric physical plane – The subtle plane (range of frequencies) closest to the dense physical plane. This plane mirrors our dense physical plane. More and more individuals, especially children, can see into this realm and see the inhabitants, including fairies and the like, who live there.

The etheric lies between the vibrational frequency of the dense physical and the vibrational frequency of the astral.

Global Network of Light – A network of light that encircles the Earth. It was introduced in the Spring 2017 issue of the WeSeekToServe.com Panel Discussions. Lightworkers are asked to do two things: send light to this network and take steps to contact other lightworkers in order to strengthen both the etheric and the physical plane network of light. The brighter the etheric network, the easier it is for the Ascended Masters to draw more light to Earth.

New Civilization / New World - The environment for the human family that will emerge as the vibrational frequency of the planet itself rises. This rise in frequency is called the shift because all who live on/in/with the planet must also raise individual and group frequency to keep pace.

The New Civilization might be summed up by the four freedoms articulated by United States President Franklyn D. Roosevelt:
- Freedom of speech
- Freedom of worship
- Freedom of want
- Freedom from fear.

As these freedoms begin full implementation for the entire human family, the New Civilization is being constructed.

Off-Earth Allies – Those beings from off Earth who have pledged support to Earth's Community of Masters and the evolution of the human family of Earth.

The Shift - The rise in frequency of planet Earth. All who live on/in/with the planet must also raise their individual and group frequency to keep pace. There is much to be learned of the shift with a Google search. Master Teachers from on and off Earth address the topic in messages published on the Master Teachers' team site WeSeekToServe.com and on Master Teacher Yeshua's website ThoughtsFromAMaster.com.

soul – A swirling potential built around a central core that is a spark of the Creator of this universe. That spark is ever and always the center, the heart of a soul. Always.

That central spark contains qualities of the Creator to be expressed throughout the universe as this soul travels. As experience accumulates, there is increased swirling around that central spark.

The soul is the totality of the spark and the swirling experiences.

Printed in Great Britain
by Amazon